French Harding

Captain, C. S. A.
Virginia's 31st Infantry & 20th Cavalry

Civil War Memoirs

May 1861-May 1865

"In the evening [I] went over to the 31st Va. and chatted awhile with the boys from Randolph Co.; those I knew on Valley Mt. **They are a noble set of fellows and fight finely**."

Jedediah Hotchkiss
Diary, April 8, 1863

Most of the Battles or Skirmishes in which French Harding participated

Location	Dates	Comments
	1861	Joins 31st VA Infantry
Laurel Hill	July 6-12	
Corrick's Ford	July 13	
Valley Mt. Campaign	Aug 15-20	Typhoid Fever
	1862	
McDowell	May 7-8	Intercepts flanking move
Front Royal	May 23	
First Winchester	May 25	
Cross Keys	June 8	
Port Republic	June 9	31st VA has 50% casualties
Richmond (Gaines' Mill)	June 27	
Richmond (Malvern Hill)	July 1	
Cedar Mountain	August 9	Leads rally w/Flag
Groveton	August 28	Hat shot off
Second Manassas	August 29-30	Close calls Brother George dies
Chantilly/Ox Hill	September 1	Shot in left shoulder
Elkwater	October 10	Brother Marion killed
Fredericksburg	December 13	Reprimanded for charging
	1863	
Imboden's WV raid	April	Shoots Sheriff Phares
Second Winchester	June 13	
Gettysburg	July 1-4	
Mine Run	Nov	Arrested
	1864	Joins 20th VA Cavalry
Chasing Gen. Hunter	June	
Salem	June	First cavalry charge
Monocacy	July 9	
Rockville	July 13	Makes charge w/o weapons
Rutherford's Farm (Stephenson's Depot)	July 20-24	Disobeys orders and leads charge
Shepherdstown	Aug 25	
Smithfield	Aug 28	His sabre against a pistol
Bunker Hill	Sep 3	Recovers Gene Hutton's body
Third Winchester	Sep 19	
Fisher's Hill	Sep 22	
Woodstock	October 9	Temporarily captured
	1865	
Huttonsville	Feb	Recovers Capt. Hill
Knapp's Creek	April 18	Fires his last shot

Captain Joseph French Harding, C. S. A.
Ca. late 1862
(Harding was wounded in the left shoulder at Ox Hill
on September 1, 1862)

Dedication

To John M. Ashcraft, Jr.
Author of the *31st Virginia Infantry*
and
All Civil War Soldiers, especially the Young men from the Huttonsville Academy who enlisted in Company F, 31st Virginia Infantry

From ON THE SLAIN COLLEGIANS by Herman Melville (1866)

Youth is the time when hearts are large,
And stirring wars
Appeal to the spirit which appeals in turn
To the blade it draws.
If woman incite, and duty show
(Though made the mask of Cain),
Or whether it be Truth's sacred cause,
Who can aloof remain
That shares youth's ardor, uncooled by the snow
Of wisdom or sordid gain?

The liberal arts and nurture sweet
Which give his gentleness to man—
Train him to honor, lend him grace
Through bright examples meet—
That culture which makes never wan . . .
[but gives] bravery to the heart; what troops
Of generous boys in happiness thus bred—
Saturnians through life's Tempe led,
Went from the North and came from the South,
With golden mottoes in the mouth,
To lie down midway on a bloody bed.
Woe for the homes of the North,
And woe for the seats of the South:
All who felt life's spring in prime,
And were swept by the wind of their place and time—
All lavish hearts, on which ever side,
Of birth urbane or courage high,
Armed them for the stirring wars—
Armed them—some to die. . . .
Warred one for Right, and one for Wrong?
So put it; but they both were young—
Each grape to his cluster clung,
All their elegies are sung. . . . .

French Harding

Civil War Memoirs

Edited with an Afterword by

Victor L. Thacker

McClain Printing Company, Inc.
Parsons, WV 26287

International Standard Book Number 0-87012-642-3
Library of Congress Catalog Card Number 00-135760
Printed in the United States of America
Copyright © 2000 by Victor L. Thacker
Elkins, WV 26241
All Rights Reserved
2000

Reprinted 2001

Typeset in Bookman Old Style
Cover artwork by Dennis L. Johnson, *The Photo Magician*
Published by McClain Printing Company
(800) 654-7179
http://McClainPrinting.com

Also visit http://FrenchHarding.com for more information
on Harding and the Civil War in West Virginia

Contents

List of Illustrations

Maps

Textual Note

This is the first published edition of French Harding's *Civil War Memoirs,* and it is based on a photocopy (presumably of the original). The photocopy is of a 220 page, double-spaced, typewritten manuscript. The location of the original (and whether or not it was first written by hand) is unknown to the family members who possess this photocopy.

The narrative is written in a style common to the turn-of-the-century Victorians, with some very long paragraphs and a heavy use of compound-complex sentences. For clarity and emphasis, a few of the longest paragraphs have been broken into smaller ones, and some punctuation has been modified to make it easier for readers to follow. But the sentence structure remains basically as Harding wrote it, because it reveals the rigor of his fine mind. There is no title page with the photocopy; but the chapter headings, with Roman numerals and descriptive sub-titles, were presumably created by Harding because they are sometimes in first person. For space considerations, the sub-titles in the Contents were abbreviated by the editor.

In the Memoirs, parentheses ( ) are Harding's, and editorial insertions are marked by brackets [ ]. The same is true for the Diary and Letter. Where possible, Harding's references to poetry and dramas are identified in footnotes.

Acknowledgements

I am grateful to Ellis S. (Bucky) Frame, III (great grandson of French Harding) and his family for permission to publish these memoirs. Without their enthusiasm for this project, this wonderful story would have remained unavailable to the public. Others who have contributed information to, advice about, and/or encouragement for the making of this book are W. Lesser Hunter and Donald L. Rice, historians from Randolph County, WV; Richard L. Armstrong, author of *19th and 20th Virginia Cavalry*, who read this manuscript; and John M. Ashcraft, Jr., author *of 31st Virginia Infantry*, who supplied most of the photographs in this book. Many thanks go to Madeline Crickard of the Allegheny Regional Family History Society in Beverly, WV, and the staffs at the West Virginia and Regional History Collection of West Virginia University; the West Virginia Department of Culture and History in Charleston, WV; the National Archives; the Ellen S. Brockenbrough Library of the Museum of the Confederacy; and the Virginia Historical Society. Michelle Mullenax, a former student of mine and vice president of McClain Printing, became my mentor for the publication process. Finally, I would like to acknowledge the support of my family: my mother, Helena Antorietto Thacker; my late father, Victor Harding Thacker; and my wife, Mary T. who said, "Get a hobby before you retire." Since then she has endured—with great good humor—visits to Port Republic, Camp Allegheny, Ox Hill (in the rain, just like the battle), and other more exciting spots. But—she is with me.

Chapter I

MY FIRST TASTE OF WAR
AS A SCOUT—AS A SENTINEL

Company F of the Thirty-first Virginia Infantry, which I joined at the outbreak of the war and with which my fortunes were linked until 1864, was organized at Huttonsville, Virginia, May 25, 1861 by the election of the following officers: Jacob Currence, captain; Jacob I. Hill, first lieutenant; George W. Salisbury, second lieutenant; Newton J. Potts, third lieutenant. Some of the boys refused office on account of their inexperience in war matters.

Colonel Porterfield, who had been assigned to the command of all the Confederate forces in Northwestern Virginia, was then at Grafton with a squad of undrilled—almost unarmed—men; their most effective weapon being muskets changed from flint to percussion locks.

On the afternoon of June 2, we marched to Beverly and camped in and about the old brick court-house, staying there until next morning when we moved to Dotson Run where we ate our first genuine army dinner, which had been prepared for our mess by "Aunt Tena" Ward; and I remember distinctly that among other good things there was a large boiled country ham—a sight of which later in the war would have been almost equal to a sight of the New Jerusalem. Dinner over and the dishes washed we proceeded on our way towards Philippi, where we had heard cannonading in the early morning; arriving where the city of Elkins now stands at four o'clock in the afternoon. Here we met the advance of Porterfield's retreating command, represented by Count [Captain?] Stofer of Huntersville, Virginia, who seemed to think that it was very probable he was the only one of the command still in the land of the living. However, we gallantly continued our forward march until we arrived at the forest on the north side of Leading Creek. Here we again discovered some suspicious looking men rapidly approaching us and took to the hillside, and William H. Wilson—afterwards lieutenant—and I undertook to ensconce ourselves behind the same tree, which we found somewhat small for that purpose. In the meantime the men who were the innocent cause of our action arrived and proved to be the head of Colonel Porterfield's command, and there was no trouble in persuading us to return with it to Huttonsville, where we arrived late in the evening of June 6, bringing up the rear and going into camp where Mill Creek now stands, having, however, left a small detachment at and near Beverly.

Shortly after night-fall a report reached our commander that the Federals were advancing upon Huttonsville from Buckhannon by the Yankee road which wound through the forests of Middle Fork and intersected the Staunton and Parkersburg Pike near our camp; and volunteers were called for to make a scout on that road to ascertain the facts. At that time I was wholly unacquainted with that section which was very sparsely settled and intersected with bypaths of which the Yankee road itself was one; but I volunteered to go provided I was furnished with a horse and guide. Both were furnished and our start at once made. My guide was a resident of that vicinity, but was not then, nor did he afterward become, a soldier; but notwithstanding that fact he lead off through the darkness right gallantly; but alas! and alack! just as our path struck the foot of Rich Mountain, he was taken suddenly and unaccountably with a severe cramp under his vest which called for his immediate return to the camp and doctor. On account of his suffering, of course, I was inclined to accompany him, but he said he thought he could make it, and he did, while I pursued my melancholy and lonely way up and across the mountain. Our instructions had been to proceed to the ford across Middle Fork River, at the mouth of Laurel Branch, some five miles from camp, and remain there, unless attacked by the enemy, until morning, and I cautiously advanced to the point designated. It was a long road but like all temporal things had an end, and I found myself on the bank of the river, where, notwithstanding I had never before noticed the similarity, I had much trouble in determining whether the noise I heard resulted from the ripple of flowing water or from the advance of a large body of cavalry, and was only able to come to a tolerably satisfactory conclusion by the actions of my horse.

I valiantly held my position through the long night; sitting most of the time on my horse for fear that if I dismounted and haste should become necessary I might lose some valuable time in recovering my seat in the saddle; and while I dozed some, so sitting, yet on account of the similarity in the sounds mentioned I, at no time, actually slept; and it is very probable that I never greeted daylight with as much pleasure, or thought the dawn so beautiful, as upon that morning; the coming of which ended my lonely vigil of a night undisturbed by the advent of any enemy more dangerous than my own vivid imagination.

With a wonderful sense of relief coupled with much elation for the doings of the night, I returned to camp over the same road I had traversed the night before, which, however, had apparently changed considerably both in looks and length.

Upon reaching the suburbs of camp, my inner man began to take note of the fact that it had been a long time since he had taken any refreshments and I stopped with my friend, Solomon Warner, for breakfast. I do not remember just what I said about my trip as scout, but doubtless I spoke of it in the best light possible to myself — probably somewhat boastfully; anyway just before I left Mr. Warner asked, "French, what would you have done if the Yankees had come?" I replied that I did not know. "Well I do," he said, "You would have run like hell"; and thinking it over later, I concluded I would have done so both from inclination and a sense of duty.

4 French Harding

From July 6 to the 12th, 1861, our Confederate command under General Garnett confronted that of the Federals under General Morris at Belington, Virgina, now West Virginia, and during that time skirmishing between them, with slight loss, was almost continuous. Shortly after midnight on the 8th, I think, the firing on our line of pickets, just west of the pike was so unusually heavy that our company was ordered to the front in consequence. The firing ceased before we arrived at our picket upon the pike, where we found several of our officers, who concluded to place an additional sentinel at some distance in advance of where we were. I was detailed for the purpose, and Adjutant Giddings [Gittings] conducted me to the position I was to occupy. That was the longest quarter-of-a-mile, as I remember it, that I ever traveled. I had heard that one of our sentinels had been killed near there the preceding night and the adjutant explained the manner of his death by telling me that he was shot by Yankee scouts, who deceived him by advancing upon his post slowly ringing a cow-bell as if it were really carried by a cow; all of which added much to the length of our walk. When we reached its end we found a few of our men there, who had been forwarded because of the alarm caused by the firing mentioned—something foreknown to the adjutant but not to me—or possibly our walk would have seemed much shorter. Be that as it may, the post I was to occupy was on the pike at the top of the hill south of Belington with the enemy north and our men south of me. There was a fenced field on my left with the corner, at which I was to stand, on the pike, while adjoining it on the north and extending towards Belington there was a wooded ridge which, in the light of what I knew and had heard from the adjutant, looked awfully foreboding to me. Nevertheless, all my comrades returned to our command and I was left there alone. To say that I felt uneasy only would be stating the fact in the most flattering manner, to myself, possible.

I stood there in the shade of that fence corner for what seemed to me almost an interminable time—eyes and ears painfully alert—when the unmistakable clank of a cow-bell was borne by the night wind, from the opposite side of the ridge mentioned, upon my startled hearing; breaking upon the awful stillness with apparent nearness and suddenness. If I could have run without anyone learning of it, probably I would have done so. I certainly felt like it; but as I could not, I had to decide what was the next best thing to do under the circumstances. I remembered reading of some of the adventures of Kenton, Wetzel and others with the Indians and determined to follow one of their devices, which I thought might be successful if but few Yankees were with the bell, which Giddings told me had been the case the night before when the sentinel was killed. Using a stake at the fence corner mentioned, with my blanket and hat, I built around it a figure which I thought would, in the darkness and at a short distance, represent a man sufficiently well to attract the attention and draw the fire of my approaching enemies. Having done so, and still keeping the pike in view, I slipped up the hill some twenty yards in the direction they were approaching and ensconced myself on the near side of a large log lying parallel to the hillside, and there waited, my old remodeled flint-lock musket cocked and protruding over that log. They took their time, imitating the motions of a cow to perfection, slowly zigzagging over and down the hill towards my position. From the noise made I thought there must be at least half a dozen of them and my only hope was to surprise and scare them. Arriving at the log some distance to my left they paused, and I supposed they had discovered my handmade man; but they turned and walked along the upper side of the log towards me, still ringing the bell, until they emerged from the darkness but a few feet from the muzzle of my waiting gun. When lo and behold, instead of the men I waited for, there burst upon my startled vision the most beautiful old cow I had ever beheld. She looked to me to be perfect in every respect, and I rejoiced with an exceeding great joy because I was not required to kill my fellowmen and for other good and sufficient reasons—known to myself.

CHAPTER II

GARNETT'S RETREAT AND
ALLEGED BATTLE OF CORRICK'S FORD

As a result of the battle of Rich Mountain, fought in his rear, General R. S. Garnett, with his command of about 3,500 men of all arms, on the night of July 11, 1861, retreated from Laurel Hill, where for some time he had been facing the Federals under General Thomas A. Morris, with about an equal force, and arrived at the intersection of the Leading Creek and Buffalo Creek Turnpike with the Beverly and Fairmont Turnpike, on the line of his retreat, at daylight on the 12th. At that time his proper route, which was by the way of Beverly and Huttonsville, was open, but acting upon information to the contrary he turned northward up the first named pike, followed it as far as the village of New Interest, and thence by a country road by way of Corrick's Ford and Horse Shoe Run to the Red House on the Northwestern Pike in Maryland, which was the only other available route. As a command, we fasted on the 12th, and camped that night at Kalar's Ford on Cheat River, in Tucker County. Sometime in the night a report reached us that the Federal General, C. W. Hill, was collecting his army to "cut us off," at the Red House; and because of such report we were ordered to, and did, continue our retreat early on the morning of the 13th, breakfastless, and before skirmishing commenced between our rear and the advance of Morris' command.

It has been claimed that Morris followed us with but 3,000 men whose rations were fully as short as ours. If true, which we very much doubt, there must have been criminal neglect or gross incompetence on his part; for assuredly, when he started he had men in greater numbers and food in greater quantity, backed by greater means, than did General Garnett. The writer had no part in the so called battle of Corrick's Ford except as a spectator. At the time it occurred his company was with its regiment over three miles distant on its way to the Red House, while he, at his request, by permission of his captain, remained with the Twenty-third Regiment, Virginia Infantry, commanded by Colonel W. B. Taliaferro, which alone fought that rearguard action. The Twelfth Georgia Regiment* did not take the part therein generally attributed to it; but notwithstanding, it was composed of as brave a body of men as ever existed, yet for some unexplained reason, it took up a line of retreat different from that of the residue of the command, almost immediately from its camp of the preceding night. I remained with the Twenty-third Regiment during the skirmishing later known as "The Battle of Corrick's Ford." The principal part of this skirmish occurred at a ford in Cheat River about three-fourths of a mile above Corrick's Ford, proper. Probably I was somewhat excited or scared while the fighting was in progress at said upper ford, but I do not remember to have seen the accurate shooting with its resulting fatal effect officially reported by the respective commanders of the contestants; and certain it is that for some reason, possibly attributable to distance instead of something less commendable, I made no use of my flintlock musket—loaded with its ball and three buckshot. Upon leaving this position most of our men retreated by the main road crossing the river at that point and re-crossing it again at Corrick's Ford; there uniting with a few who had followed a trail down the west side of the river, and near there meeting General Garnett, whom I last saw within fifteen minutes of the time when, and within two hundred yards of where, he was killed while leading his men in a skirmish. From this point the Federals did not follow us; or if they did they remained out of sight and gave us no further trouble. Of the losses

---

* This should be the First Georgia. The Twelfth did not actually join Garnett. It reached the Greenbrier River and met the remnants of the Rich Mountain Force retreating.

incurred at Corrick's Ford, I can not speak from personal knowledge, further than as above given, except to say that several of the number reported by Colonel Taliaferro as killed or badly wounded turned up with the Georgians when we met them in Dixie after the retreat—as I remember it, over half the number he so reported. I spent about three weeks in the winter of 1865-6 at Corrick's Ford at the home of the genial "Uncle Billy" Corrick, then the head of the Corrick family, and he told me that neither army lost in killed over eight or ten men, and the Confederates who were killed there, with the exception of General Garnett, were buried on his farm.

But for the fact that General C. W. Hill was collecting his 6,000 Federals at the Red House on our only line of retreat, we would have had no trouble with General Morris at Corrick's Ford; the trouble would have been the other way around, for certainly we were not afraid of Morris, nor did we make any haste or lose any equipment because he was following us. Our whole effort was to forestall General Hill. We first learned on the afternoon prior to going into camp at Kalar's that he was ordered to cut us off at St. George, which we knew would be impossible; but some time that night, prior to the time skirmishing between Morris' advance and our pickets commenced, we learned that the effort to intercept us was to be made at the Red House—something quite possible of accomplishment; and we were ordered to move immediately. The culpability of the would-be historian who, in the face of the facts, undertakes to inculcate in the minds of his readers the idea that because of the doings of General Morris and his troops, the command of General Garnett was routed, demoralized, or in any way hurried upon its retreat, can only be excused, if at all upon the ground of gross ignorance. Our trouble was in front not in the rear.

Unmolested we passed the Red House early on the morning of the 14th, after having marched all night—still without food. Some makers of history allege that General Hill did not undertake to intercept us at that point because he had been unable to collect a sufficient number of his men there to successfully meet us, which is probably true for we were desperately hungry, and would have fought furiously for something to eat, if for nothing else; but be that as it may, a considerable number of his men were in sight when we arrived there and a part, or all, of our regiment was formed in a heavy skirmish line and advanced west and north of that point a short distance, where we faced a similar line of the enemy, except that, to us, it appeared to be much heavier than our own; but possibly it was magnified by the dimness of the morning light aided by a more vivid imagination. However, we remained in that position until the residue of our command had all passed the Red House, when we were ordered to follow it eastward for some distance on the Northwestern Pike and thence by country roads to Monterey in Highland County, Virginia, where we arrived, as I remember it, on the 17th of July, foot-sore and hungry but in reasonably good spirits, which a few days later were further raised by the news of the fight at Manassas.

My comrades, as well as myself, learned by actual experience on this retreat that I could fast longer and run faster than any other man in old Company F, because when we arrived at Monterey I was carrying the muskets of two of them, as well as my own, and was, on account of my better physical condition, immediately detailed for duty ahead of my regular turn. I retained my reputation, as the fastest runner, until the close of the war.

On our retreat we camped one night in Pendleton County, I think, after most of us had been marching some sixty hours practically without food. I was very hungry and discovering a farm-house at no great distance hastened there at once. Others had been before me, but the kind old mistress, apologizing by saying she had but little more to offer, placed upon the table before me about half of a large pone, freshly baked, and enough delicious butter and butter-milk, freshly churned, to satisfy two hungry men, which I attacked so voraciously that by the time I had eaten a very few bites such a quarrel arose between the food and my empty stomach that I was compelled to quit and return to camp, where I arrived just about as hungry as when I left it. All of which our doctor said resulted from the gormandizing manner in which I bolted the food.

Another incident which exercised a controlling influence over all my after-life occurred on this retreat, at the village of New Interest on the 12th day of July. I was at that time unacquainted with the people residing there, but my brother, Marion, had taught school in that vicinity and was acquainted with them. Breakfastless and weary we arrived there about noon, and while halted for a brief rest in the street the kind people came out to the side-walk with such food as they still had on hand and generously distributed it among us. With others came the beautiful little twelve-year-old girl who later became my darling wife. We were standing at her father's gate and she handed the food she had brought to Marion for distribution. He told me who she was. It was our first meeting, and our command immediately marched away leaving her standing there, a vision of purity and loveliness, and I did not see her again until after the close of the war; but I never forgot, nor will I ever forget, the little girl we left behind us standing at the Wilmoth gate.

CHAPTER III

WITH GENERAL LEE AT VALLEY MOUNTAIN

A few days after we arrived at Monterey upon our retreat from Laurel Hill we were marched to Camp Alleghany where we remained until about the 12th of August. At this camp not less than forty of our company had the measles. Indeed very few who were present for duty escaped. I was one of the few, but I had a time nursing the other fellows. However, good old Mother Yeager, upon whose husband's land we were camped, taught me how to make tea out of an herb that grew wild upon their farm, the name of which I do not now remember, but the effect of a few doses of which, when taken by the boys in proper quantities, was almost magical, and in no case, where used, did the disease prove fatal. From this camp our company was detached from its regiment and ordered to Valley Mountain, in this county, where we arrived, as I remember it, about the 15th of August—having left a few boys who had not fully recovered from the measles at Camp Alleghany. It was here that I first saw General R. E. Lee. I then thought, as I still think, that he was the finest looking man, both in features and figure, I had ever seen; and when a day or two later I visited his headquarters tent in company with our captain, Jacob Currence, (where the latter had been summoned to discuss the advisability of sending a scouting party to the rear of General Reynold's position to procure information of the situation), I obtained an insight to that dignified graciousness which constituted one of his greatest charms. As a result of this conference Captain Currence, taking with him Lieutenant George W. Salisbury, Dudley Long, brother Marion and myself, immediately proceeded to make the trip indicated, going by the way of Point Mountain, now Monterville, thence to the head of and down Mill Creek, to where the town by that name now stands, and where the captain then resided. Here we camped in the woods a short distance from the Currence Mill for two nights and a day, when, after obtaining all the information possible in relation to numbers of, and positions occupied by, the enemy in that vicinity, we at once returned to camp by the way we had come, except we went by Cowger's Mill and up Dry Branch, having spent but five days in making the trip, which resulted satisfactorily, as reported by the captain.

Neither Captain Currence nor myself performed any further service during the Valley Mountain Campaign. Each of us was taken with a severe case of typhoid fever immediately upon our return to camp, from which neither recovered until our army had fallen back to Marlin's Bottom—now Marlinton, on [the] Greenbrier river; to which we were hauled in an ambulance. While sick at Valley Mountain I was kindly taken into the home of, and cared for by Mr. 'Gustus Wood and family, with whom I had theretofore been but slightly acquainted; and my own family could not have nursed me better or treated me more kindly than they. It resulted in the beginning of a lifelong friendship. I was delirious or semi-delirious nearly all the time I remained there, and, therefore, do not have a very distinct recollection of the passing military events; but do remember having some trouble with my doctor, D. B. Lang when upon hearing the army marching by "Uncle" Gus's house I, in some way become cognizant of the fact that General Lee was advancing. I also remember throwing my boot at the doctor when he undertook to give me a drink of water with whiskey in it. I had not then, nor have I yet, knowingly tasted any intoxicant. I know that General Lee's West Virginia campaign has, by some, been pronounced a failure, to which he, as a general contributed. I do not so consider it when viewed in the light of all the circumstances. Doubtless he accomplished all that was expected of him. So far as we have ever learned, all the official information we have, as to General Lee's object in coming to Western Virginia, is contained in a letter, dated August 1, 1861 from President Davis to General Johnston, found on pages 766-7 of Vol. 5, Series 1, of the Official Records of The War of The Rebellion, in which the President says: "General Lee has gone to Western Virginia, and I hope may be able to strike a decisive blow at the enemy in that quarter; or, failing in that, will be able to organize and post our troops so as to check the enemy, after which he will return to this place." And, not withstanding the fertile imagination of some would-be historians, the above is the only foundation whereon they built.

The line which General Lee was to look over, or act upon, as he thought best, was about two hundred miles in length, extended from Kentucky through the mountains of Western Virginia to the Maryland line, and, for the greater distance, was peopled by a hostile population. It was far removed from all bases of supplies with almost impassable intervening roads. When he arrived at Valley Mountain, late in August, he found it defended by a comparatively small, inharmonious and scattered army—wholly unprovided with the necessary equipment to keep it in the field. He further found that the enemy occupying and advancing upon said line not only outnumbered his army but was much better equipped for war, in every respect, except in gallantry. He found facing him, at and in reach of Elk Water and Cheat Mountain when he advanced in September, an effective force of from 12,000 to 14,000 Federal soldiers, immediately under the command of General Reynolds; while at that time, General Rosecrans occupied the region of the Kanawha Valley, with an additional available force of not less than 23,00O men; and both of these Federal commands were then in easy reach of others from which they could be readily reinforced.

These numbers were taken from the Record of the War of the Rebellion, (usually unreliable, but occasionally correct in its abstracts of army numbers). However, in this instance the number of men here credited to General Reynolds was verified by our scout above mentioned. On the other hand there is no respectable authority extant which credits General Lee with as great a number of men, or with an equally good equipment. Nor did he have them subject to his orders.

Unquestionably Colonel Rust's proposed attack on the enemy on Cheat Mountain, (no matter whether planned by General Lee or by General Loring before the arrival of the former, as we then thought), resulted in complete failure; but whether such failure or the wonderful military prescience of General Lee led to his retirement from Valley Mountain was then left to the future to decide. His own version of the situation as expressed, at the time, to our comrades, Captain Marshall and Lieutenant Perry Lewis, who guided him to and in the rear of the enemy's position at Elk Water (and who communicated it to the writer soon thereafter), was that, while he thought he could still succeed in his attack, yet, on account of the remoteness of that section from all his bases of supplies; the almost impossibility of transporting them over the intervening bad roads with the means at his command; the scarcity of provision to be found in the territory then occupied, and recently foraged over, by the enemy, who would, for reasons similar to his own, most likely abandon their advanced positions or move forward where they could be more easily met and disastrously defeated; all augmented by the hostility of the people around and in front of us, the advantages to be gained, even by success, would not be commensurate with the losses which must necessarily occur by such an attack. How well General Lee's foresight, as so expressed, was sustained, with its accompanying advantages, by the battles of Greenbrier River, of Camp Alleghany, of McDowell, of those fought in the Shenandoah Valley in which these western troops took a part, and in later developments showing the utter impossibility of our holding Western Virginia, needs no comment here. History speaks for itself; and those who, thoughtlessly or ignorantly, adversely criticised General Lee's management of this campaign, stand condemned in the light of after events, while he stands vindicated absolutely, with his fame as a thoughtful and successful general unsullied. He unquestionably maneuvered his army in the Gauley section, before the superior force of General Rosecrans, in such manner as to compel the latter to retreat and go into winter quarters near Gauley Bridge; thereby accomplishing the alternative object of his campaign, namely: checking the enemy.

CHAPTER IV

SCOUTING LIFE

From about September 23, 1861, until the latter part of March, 1862, with the exception of January 3rd and 4th, our company—still on detached service—camped at Huntersville, Virginia, under the command of a Tennesseean, I think, whose name and rank I do not recall. For the two excepted days, our commander generously allowed Major Wheeler with a much larger Federal force, to occupy that point somewhat to the detriment of our very small stock of commissary and quartermaster supplies; returning, however, as soon as the latter left. While our company was stationed there, the residue of our regiment took part in the battles of Greenbrier River and Camp Alleghany. While so camped at Huntersville our discipline was very slack, and some of us, under the guise of scouting, were allowed to go and come almost at will, and we went and came accordingly. Indeed so long as the direction we took was toward the enemy, which in our case was toward home, we were encouraged to go; in consequence of which I spent much of the period named in our home county of Randolph and in going to and returning from it to camp, and it is of some of these trips, most interesting to myself, I now write.

Late in September, going by the way of Clover Lick, Big Springs, Valley Mountain and the western face of Cheat Mountain, and keeping in or near the roads or paths, my brother Marion and I paid a visit to the Huttonsville community (then occupied by the Federal forces), where we had both attended school before the war, having resided near there at that time. Consequently we were well acquainted with both the people and country in that vicinity, and notwithstanding its occupation by the

16

army of General Reynolds, we had a splendid time visiting our friends and girl schoolmates, most of whose gentlemen friends were then with our army; and the fact that we were within the enemy's lines only gave additional spice to our pleasures. To their number, I do not believe that any community then occupying "God's Green Earth" could out-rival that of Huttonsville in the intelligence, kindness, goodness and beauty of its girls—especially of its Dixie girls; and we stayed at and in the vicinity of Huttonsville about a week, intending at the end of that tine to visit our home near where the city of Elkins now stands. But on the evening of October 1st, I think, we learned that a certain gentleman residing on the back road, which ran from the Mill Creek bridge by the way of the Scott ford and his home to Beverly, was expecting Colonel Milroy to take supper with him late on the next day, which would doubtless make him re-cross the Scott ford after dark, and whether practicable or not, Marion and I concluded that if he returned alone, as was expected, we would capture him at the ford and take him South. We remained in sight of the road at that point on the evening he was expected, until it was so late that we knew he would fail to keep his appointment; and we learned soon after leaving it that on that morning General Reynolds had advanced from Cheat Mountain to Greenbrier River where the battle of the 3rd occurred, and we set down the Colonel's failure to come to that movement. However while waiting for him at the ford, late in the evening a United States wagon loaded with beef hides and drawn by two splendid United States horses crossed the river and stopped for the night at the house where the Colonel had intended to sup; leaving his wagon, with his horses eating out of the trough swinging at its rear, standing in the road at the barn-yard gate, as if to tempt the cupidity of near-by rebels; of all of which we immediately became cognizant, and concluded that it would be no bad exchange to capture two first class horses instead of one fourth class colonel, which we did in the following manner:

After taking supper with our sister who lived near-by and waiting until the lights in the vicinity were all extinguished, we cautiously approached the place occupied by the wagon and horses and found them still there. We first untied the horses and led them a short distance away by their halters. We were not sure whether their driver was sleeping at the house or in the wagon. If in the wagon he might have heard us, kept quiet through fear, and would give the alarm as soon as we left. Therefore we concluded to ascertain how this matter stood, and Marion held the horses while I explored the wagon, finding the horses' bridles but no man, and we went on our way satisfied. Going northward on the road a short distance, we turned off upon a plat of sod, thence by an unused path to Shaver's Run where we looked up our old friend, Adam McGee, who guided us by a way entirely trackless after crossing Cheat Mountain, to a point known as Dent's Cabin on the east face of the mountain, near the present site of Wildell, in Pocahontas county. We arrived at Dent's Cabin on the evening of the 4th, having heard the cannonading at Greenbrier River on our way. Here our guide left us, and we proceeded by the way of the Upper Sinks to Hightown in Highland County, Virginia, where a considerable force was encamped. (Here we sold our horses for two hundred dollars in gold.) We handed most of this money to Father upon arriving at home a few days later.

When we next visited Huttonsville, we learned that the disappearance of these horses was charged to two deserters, who left the Federal army at Huttonsville that night.

After disposing of our horses, as above mentioned, instead of going on to Huntersville we again started on our homeward way; retraced our route to Upper Sinks, and thence home by paths well known to us. Here a welcome, such as only loving parents and sisters could bestow, awaited us. This was the first time we had been there since we passed by on Garnett's retreat Therefore, our homecoming was very pleasant, rendered less so, perhaps, by the fact that a small detachment of Federal soldiers was encamped nearby, which, added to the knowledge that some of our nearest neighbors were in sympathy with them, kept Mother very uneasy, and us practically concealed from outsiders, while we stayed there for about a week.

Then bidding our loved ones good-bye, we started back to Huntersville by the way of Huttonsville. It was now near the middle of October. We started about daylight, took the trails east of the main road and reached the Kelly Mountain road, at a point near the old Baptist Meeting-house, about 10 o'clock in the morning, just as a wagon train, in charge of a quartermaster, was passing on its way to said mountain after forage. We were armed, and dressed in our usual clothing. The captain dismounted, and we sat down by the roadside together, and had a pleasant talk of considerable length, while his train moved by and on. He was quite talkative but by no means inquisitive, and we obtained some useful information, but said and did nothing that could brand us as spies, notwithstanding we hewed pretty close to that line. After leaving him we continued on our way, still by trails leading east of the main road, and arrived, shortly before sunset on top of the first hill south of Shaver's Run, from where we could look down on the home of young Andrew Wamsley, fronting on the main road. By now we felt ready for supper, and seeing "Andy" standing in his doorway, cautiously communicated that fact to him. In the shortest time possible, he was with us with a basket containing a supper, which his excellent wife, Martha, had prepared, fit for two kings. While eating it, he informed us that there was to be an apple-cutting at his house that night, which would be attended by several of the young people of the neighborhood, as well as by some of the Federal soldiers then encamped just across the river, and the question of whether or not Marion and I could be concealed so as to safely attend, arose. Andy was in favor of the project at once, saying that the room to be used was large; that one corner of it was occupied by an old-fashioned bedstead, to which was suspended a valance which completely hid the space under the bedding; and that he was sure that no one would attempt to explore that space. We demurred at first, not so much on our own account as on his. He said that the Yankees had given him so much trouble already that if any mishap occurred he would go to Dixie with us. His wife was then consulted and found to be not only willing but anxious to see the plan carried out. We agreed, foolishly perhaps, and in a very short time were reclining on a stuffed quilt under that bed, having first told Mrs. Wamsley to let certain of our lady friends know we were there and would be pleased to, later, have the privilege of escorting them home. Shortly after night-fall the young people, who lived nearby commenced to arrive and continued to come until a goodly number, together with some twelve or fifteen Federal soldiers, were assembled in that room, where they remained until they had peeled, cut and strung all the apples on hand. They then proceeded to "Strip The Willow," occasionally kicking that valance almost in our faces as we peeped from under it. It was a gay crowd, full of young life, and to say that we enjoyed the situation, immensely, would be putting it mildly. We apprehended no danger, whatever. The soldiers had stacked their guns in a remote corner of the room, while ours were within easy reach. Our most trouble arose from an inclination to cough, and to prevent that we successfully ate gunpowder. So far as I can now recollect, this was the only regular apple-cutting I ever attended. After it was over and the general crowd had dispersed, we learned that Mrs. Wamsley had carried out our above indicated request. Gratefully thanking her and her gallant husband for the friendship and kindness shown us, Marion and I walked home with our friends whom we knew to be splendid Dixie girls.

This incident occurred over fifty-six years ago, and all those above named, as well as all the most intimate friends who then and there met me, and who were then full of vigorous young life, kindness, and friendship, have long since passed over the "Great Divide," while I alone am left behind.

Before the dawn of the coming morning after the apple-cutting, Marion and I started on our return to Dixie, greeting and bidding good-bye to our Huttonsville, Elk Water, and Mingo friends on our way.

CHAPTER V

A SHEEP INCIDENT

After our return from the apple-cutting expedition, Elihu Hutton, who had not then joined the army, asked me to take a trip with him to his home at Huttonsville; and together with J. R. Apperson and Asa Kelley, of Company F, we at once started. Brother Marion was tired and did not go with us. We spent the first night at McCoppin's on Clover Lick and next morning crossed Elk Mountain to the Big Springs branch of the Elk River some distance north of the Springs. The bottom there was of considerable width and partly in sod, and the path we were following crossed it to the eastern foot of Cheat Mountain where it entered the timber and abruptly turned south toward the Springs. When we were about halfway across the bottom we discovered, and were ourselves immediately seen by, a detachment of Federal soldiers coming up through the timber by the path from the Springs and about one-third of a mile distant. At first it was impossible to determine their number or whether cavalry or infantry, but we were not long left in doubt. Some of them ran out to the edge of the woods and commenced firing at us while others kept up the path in the timber, thus disclosing some 50 or 60 men in all, about 20 of whom were mounted. As soon as we made this discovery a hasty retreat to the timber at the foot of Elk Mountain, which grew north of and to the path by which we came, was suggested and acted upon.

Neither Kelley nor Apperson were used to much exertion of any kind, and the kind just then necessary was rather exhausting, so we told them to get and they got accordingly. Hutton and I who were much better runners waited until the horsemen uncovered themselves by making the turn in the path when we both emptied our guns at them and at the same time gave a weak imitation of the later celebrated Confederate yell. I do not think we hit anybody but the exposed horsemen fell back to the shelter of the timber, from which desultory firing was continuing. By this time our other boys were about half-way to the timber they sought, but were apparently going so slowly that I asked Hutton to hurry them up and he tried to do so. On account of the unevenness of the ground I do not think the enemy had yet recognized the smallness of our numbers. In the mean time I had reloaded my gun and started to retreat, and I must have done an excellent job at it for none of the boys had advanced more than twenty-five yards into the woods when I reached it and heard Hutton using some unbiblical language, more forcible than otherwise, at Kelley who appeared to be very tired and ready to stop and surrender. Hutton's cuss-words were effective, however, and Kelley again slowly moved on. About this time the leading files of the Yankee horseman who had advanced when I retreated had arrived within about one hundred and fifty yards of us, and thinking that perhaps they were in range of my unreliable gun I again shot at them. Doubtless I missed the immediate object aimed at but the shot caused some confusion in the ranks of the enemy, and for some reason they followed us no farther, and I soon joined my comrades.

I had been fearful that Kelley was wounded but found that he was only completely exhausted. Apperson was in better condition, but they were both so tired that by the time we had re-crossed Elk Mountain and gotten to Mr. Shinnaberry's on the south side of Clover Lick Run, not over four miles from where the Yankees left us, night had overtaken us. Here we had supper, and after consultation it was agreed that Hutton, who was disinclined to give up his visit home, should on the next morning return to camp with Apperson and Kelley, while I was to remain in the vicinity on the lookout for the enemy until his return. I promised to spend the night near the path leading by McCoppin's, which we had formerly followed, and report at once if I saw anything suspicious, and so we parted. My doings for the next two, or three days are, even to myself, rather uninteresting. I at once started upon the path indicated; stopped and quietly investigated McCoppin's house; found a man stretched out before the fire in the sitting room—sound asleep; watched him a short time through a broken pane of the back window, then left him there and proceeded on my way to the top of Elk Mountain from where I could overlook our battlefield of the morning. All was dark and quiet, and I blanketed and slept near the path until daylight and then returned to McCoppin's for breakfast. There I learned that the man I had seen lying before the fire was Walt Allen, who later was a rather notorious Federal scout, and who at one time took part in a plot to have me waylaid and shot without warning, as I afterward learned from some of his men.

Learning from McCoppin that Allen, who had been with the Yankees, had reported that they had all returned to Randolph I remained at and near his home until the third evening, I think, after separating from Hutton, when he, in company with Ad[am] Ward and Dud[ley] Long of Company F, arrived there, remaining over night. We started next morning by the same path before followed and arrived in sight of Amos Heavener's place in Mingo where we had intended taking dinner about noon. Finding a company of the enemy in possession of the door-yard we turned down the western face of Cheat Mountain and took the path we usually followed towards Huttonsville; and having no food, shot one of Mr. Heavener's sheep which we found grazing on the lower end of his farm. We roughly dressed it and proceeded to the head of Windy Run where we camped for the night. There we roasted and ate a very small portion of the meat, hung the residue up before the fire to roast and lay down to sleep leaving Ad to attend to it and anticipating a glorious breakfast next morning. But alas! when morning came Ad was still there as large as, or perhaps larger than, life, but that sheep had mysteriously and almost wholly disappeared—Ad said it dripped away—and we slowly and still hungry for mutton took our weary way to the head of Becca's Creek where lived our tried friend William Wamsley, at whose home we aimed to arrive just after dark. He lived on one of the paths leading from Elk Water to Cheat Mountain, both of which points were then occupied by Federal soldiers and caution was necessary. We proceeded as planned and just after dark were cautiously approaching Mr. Wamsley's house when Ward accidently [sic] stepped below the path on a steep hillside and under a walnut tree and, assisted by the walnuts, went lumbering down the hill for some distance, making a noise that could be heard for a quarter of a mile; while Hutton, releasing his pent-up wrath in unorthodox language that could have been heard at an equal distance exclaimed, "Ward, I'll be damned if I didn't know that sheep would get you down some time but I didn't know when or how." When Ad had gathered himself up and matters had quieted down, we again approached the house where we found Mr. Wamsley and his family on the porch, alone, having come out there on account of our unusual racket, and were accorded by them, as ever, a hearty welcome, given a splendid supper and sent on our way toward Huttonsville with a kindly "God speed you." We arrived at Huttonsville safely, remained there a few days among our friends, had a pleasurable time, and returned to Huntersville without further incident worthy of recording; but Ad Ward's reputation as the boss Epicurean survived the war. His reputation as a gallant soldier, one of the best, was of equal life.

CHAPTER VI

SCOUTING WITH MY CAPTAIN

About December 20, 1861, Captain Currence concluded to visit his home near Huttonsville, and asked Marion, Dud. Long and me to go with him. Apparently he had not entirely recovered from the attack of fever he had at Valley Mountain and we tried to dissuade him, upon the ground that he was unable to make the trip, but he insisted so earnestly—even pathetically—that upon the advice of his doctor we reluctantly consented. As I remember it we left camp on the afternoon of the 21st, aiming to reach Huttonsville on the evening of the 24th, thus, on account of the Captain's condition, allowing at least one day extra in which to make the trip; but even so, although we met with no hindrance whatever, we did not reach Huttonsville until the early morning of the 25th, barely seeing the Captain home in time to eat his Christmas dinner. Marion and I crossed the river above the Scott ford and took a late dinner with our sister, Margaret Smith. Before separating, however, we had made arrangements to meet Long later and go with him, to his home two miles north of the Mill Creek bridge on the pike. General Milroy was now in command at Huttonsville, instead of General Reynolds, who had been transferred to other fields of action. Milroy had fought the battle at Camp Allegheny only three or four days after his promotion, and we learned on Christmas evening that he was then contemplating some other action, but could not learn just what it was; but determined to be on the alert and if possible forestall it by reporting to General Johnson. A day or two later Dud came by and we went home with him for the night. He and the Captain had also heard that some move of the army was brewing. Marion and I had intended to go home for our New Year's dinner, but waited, and by the evening of the 28th we had mobilized our forces on the back road north of the Scott ford ready for action but still uncertain. About daylight next morning we received a reliable message that a Federal cavalry force would start for Huntersville by the way of Mingo in a day or two and that Milroy would advance, at the same time, by the Staunton and Parkersburg Pike upon Alleghany Mountain. Captain Currence vetoed a proposition to divide our force by some of us going direct to Huntersville and others to Camp Allegheny which seemed to me to be the better plan, and together, with two days rations, we started by the way of Shaver's Run and Dent's Cabin for the latter point. We ought to have made the trip in two days, but hindered by the Captain who was far from well, we did not arrive there until the afternoon of the third day. The weather was cold and rough, and when we came to Cheat River we found it over two feet deep with the mush-ice flowing on its surface. We had no time to construct a foot-log, and but little means to do so. Under the circumstances I removed my lower underclothing and socks, replaced my shoes to save my feet, rolled up my pants, shouldered the Captain, and speedily and safely carried him across the river, losing some little blood from contact with the ice, but after replacing my clothes I felt quite comfortable, and we at once moved onward.

On the second night we stayed at Mr. Van Buren Arbogast's on the eastern fork of Greenbrier River, some distance north of Camp Bartow, where General Johnson had a picket on the pike, and next morning crossed the river and reached the pike on the mountain side, about half way between the picket and Camp Alleghany; at which point we left the Captain to follow more slowly, while some of us hurried on to camp to make report. General Johnson was very much inclined to discredit our news—enough so to make us somewhat angry—but our colonel, W. L. Jackson, intervened and vouched for our veracity, and the General became convinced that we had good reason for the "faith that was in us." [He] sent a mounted courier with a dispatch to the commandant at Huntersville, the result of which I never heard, and that evening or next morning strengthened his picket at Camp Bartow. When Captain Currence reached camp that evening he was completely exhausted, and we remained there until the 5th or 6th of January—until after the descent upon, and evacuation of, Huntersville, which occurred on the 3rd. On the 2nd, as can be gathered from Johnson's correspondence with the authorities at the time, and as we then knew, the enemy appeared in force before Camp Bartow, and doubtless, was only deterred from advancing on Alleghany by learning, from seeing that the picket at Bartow had been strengthened, that he was expected and prepared for. General Johnson, whose force was much less than that of the enemy, had little or no fear of the result in case of a direct attack upon his position, but was somewhat fearful of being flanked—something that would certainly have been easy to accomplish—and why he was not remains one of the unexplained mysteries of strategic warfare.

We left Camp Alleghany with Captain Currence about the 6th of January. He was quite feeble and we traveled very slowly, and when we reached Frost on Knapp's Creek he was so ill that we left him at a Mr. Gibson's there, with brother Marion to nurse him. So far as I now remember the Captain performed no further service in the army, which he left at the expiration of the year for which he enlisted, completely broken down in health. We met our company comrades at Frost returning from Monterey to Huntersville, and Dud and I went with them. It was amusing to hear their different versions of the fall of Huntersville. Their ideas of the number of the attacking force were extremely variant, ranging from 1,000 to 5,000, and of the amount and effectiveness of the fighting done even more conflicting. The gallant W. H. Wilson, later lieutenant, was clearly of the opinion that their command could and would have repulsed the enemy and held the town had they been properly handled and allowed to fight, and later developments appeared to sustain him.

Notwithstanding the somewhat bombastic report of the Federal commander, Major Wheeler, which I once read, when divested of all rodomontade, the circumstances attending this capture of Huntersville are about as follows: Wheeler, with a force of from 800 to 1,000 well equipped cavalrymen taken from Huttonsville and Elkwater, attacked the 225 poorly equipped mixed force at Huntersville, who, after exchanging a few shots with the enemy, retreated without loss to themselves, and with but little loss to the Federals, who did not capture one-third of the stores as reported by Major Wheeler—for the rebels did not have them there to be captured.

CHAPTER VII

MY FIRST YANKEE

While camped at Huntersville, several of our company, together with some of Jo Gay's band of rangers, all under the command of the latter, scouted by the way of the head of Clover Lick toward Mingo. I do not remember the date but it was quite cold and there was some snow on the ground in the fore-part of the day. On the pike near the Big Springs we found the trail of some 25 Federal soldiers—a force fully equal to our own—going in the direction of Edray, and we immediately turned and followed them, arriving near the residence of William Gibson, who was, I think, related to Gay in some way, just after dark. From here Gay, who lived on Elk Mountain and knew the country, led us a short distance into the ridges north of the pike where he temporarily, and without noise or fire, camped his men; and in company with Rebel Jake Simmons and the writer returned to the pike for the purpose of ascertaining the whereabouts of the enemy. We first quietly investigated William Gibson's home, and saw, through a back window, Yankee Jake Simmons sitting by the fire in the living-room. I did not know him but both Gay and Rebel Jake did, and the latter would probably have shot at him had he not been restrained by Gay who opposed making any noise until we had accomplished the object for which we came. So far as we were able to ascertain, none of Yankee Jake's comrades were with him, but of this we were not sure—certainly all his company were not there. Rebel Jake now returned to camp, and Gay and I quietly proceeded on our way towards the widow Gibson's home some distance away on the pike leading to Edray. Before reaching it, thinking that possibly some few of the enemy were in our rear with Yankee Jake, we determined that Gay should remain where he was to warn me of, or protect me from, any who were following us, while I proceeded to investigate the widow's house. The snow had melted. It was quite dark and my advance was fearfully cautious. Keeping and creeping somewhat below the roadbed, I soon discovered a sentinel standing in the pike, scarcely twenty feet away, but succeeded in passing him without being seen, and made my way to an old-fashioned log wood-pile in Mrs. Gibson's door-yard. While concealed there two or three Yankees visited it for fuel and I learned from their talk not only that they were camped there for the night but that they intended to continue on their way over Elk Mountain to Edray early next morning. This was all we wanted to know and by a different way from that by which I came, I joined Gay and returned with him to camp, where a consultation as to how we should proceed ensued. About this we almost irreconcilably differed. W. H. Wilson, Cyrus Crouch, Eugene Hutton, myself and others of our company were in favor of dividing our force, placing part of it on the pike east and the residue thereof, thereon, west of the widow's house, in supporting distance of each other, and attack as soon as the enemy should move; but Gay, as commander, determined to remain where we were for the night and attack the enemy in the house at daylight next morning, and perforce we had to acquiesce. That our plan was the better we think will be conceded by all military men.

Pursuant to said arrangement we gallantly charged upon the house at daylight next morning, and the writer, at least, was very much relieved to find that the enemy had, earlier still, proceeded on their way across Elk Mountain. We followed to within a short distance of its top where a by-path, leading to Gay's home on the mountain some little distance away, intersected the pike from the north. Here Gay concluded to go by his home with most of his rangers, get breakfast and join us again farther on. While we remained at that point brother Marion walked to the top of the mountain. Just north of where the pike crossed it, a rough ridge, then in woods, ran eastwardly therefrom; and something over one hundred yards from said crossing the pike made a bend near the foot of, and in conformity with, the ridge. Immediately before we reached this crossing we met Marion returning, and he told us that he had heard the bursting of a gun cap on the ridge-side above the bend. Thoughtlessly, perhaps, W. H. Wilson, Cyrus Crouch, myself and probably one or two of the other boys exposed ourselves at the crossing on the mountain top. The moment we did so a shot, apparently coming from an old mountain rifle, rang out from that hill-side, and the ball passed close enough to Cy's head to leave an unpleasant reminder of the closeness of its passage. We later learned that this shot was fired by Yankee Jake who recognized and tried to kill Cy. Be that as it may, the skirmish was now on. As the rest of our boys arrived the enemy poured a harmless volley over them and they returned it in kind. We yelled "charge" and ran rapidly down the road while the Yankees ran as rapidly as they could up the hill from the road. After the fiasco in which I had engaged in company with Elihu Hutton and others, I had exchanged my gun for an easily handled close shooting Mississippi rifle which I now carried. I had not stopped on the mountain to shoot but when I arrived at the bend in the road, I discovered a broad-backed blue-coat scrambling up the hill some seventy-five or eighty yards distant, blazed away and knocked him over. I felt a little queer as we ran by where he lay on his face so still, but braced myself with the thought that he had voluntarily invaded our state with hostile intent and ran on, loading my gun as I went. When we reached the top of the hill we found cleared land, and the Yankees who had the advantage of a down-hill run disappearing in the distance; their hindmost man, so far as I could guess, being about three hundred yards off; and I again effectively brought my Mississippi into play; my victim this time lying down after going a few steps.

Gay who had heard our firing and was coming to us now commenced firing on the Federals who were leading their retreat, and they sheered off to the Clover Lick side of the mountain. Leaving some of our men there to take care of the wounded and bury the dead, if any, I returned, with a few friends, to where the soldier I had first shot had fallen. Upon arriving there we found his gun, blanket, shot-pouch and cap, but no blood or man. Upon a more careful examination, we discovered that from that point back to and across the road, someone's boot heel had hit the ground at intervals of about five feet, and that after topping the mountain south of the road, the boot heel impressions continued down the west side of the mountain toward the widow Gibson's, who a few days later informed the writer that the owner of the boots, the heels of which made said impressions, arrived at her house about noon the day of the fight, very hungry and minus the equipment we had found on the field of battle but otherwise unhurt and unscathed. His was a clear case of 'possum acting.

For some time previous to the occurrence of this incident I had been somewhat inclined to be boastful both of my gun and marksmanship—a fact about which the boys, thereafter, were not slow in reminding me. Indeed in common parlance they "rubbed it in." However, my second shot which, at a distance of three-hundred yards—slightly farther than the range of my gun—had caught Mr. George P. Spurgeon of Ohio in the calf of his leg, to some extent redeemed my reputation, for we saw my Mississippi rifle ball extracted from his leg where it had lodged against the bone.

As I remember it, the Federals lost one man killed and four wounded in this skirmish, while we lost none.

CHAPTER VIII

SCOUT TO MONTEREY—BATTLE OF MCDOWELL

About the last of March, 1862, we left Huntersville and joined the rest of our regiment, then encamped at the eastern foot of the Shenandoah Mountain, under the command of General Ed. Johnson. While at Huntersville our first lieutenant, Jacob I. Hill, was transferred to the quartermaster's department, and the boys had elected me to fill his place. This made very little difference in our relations.

Some time in April (I do not recollect the date), General Johnson determined to advance upon Monterey, then held by General Milroy with a reported force of some 3,000 men, and attack if deemed advisable. A day or two before starting, the General dispatched Dr. D. B. Lang and myself with a force of some 25 men—which we were to command jointly—with instructions to proceed, as best we could, to the top of the mountain between Monterey and Hightown, and guard and blockade the pike there in case Milroy should attempt to retreat thereupon. General Johnson had a company of cavalry picketed on the pike several miles west of McDowell, and anticipating no trouble until after we had passed that point, we kept [to] the pike until late in the afternoon of the day we started, and had gone through a rocky pass some distance west of McDowell when we met the captain of the cavalry company, who informed us that the Yankees were advancing in sufficient force to have compelled his retreat from his original position, but that he had taken another position some two or three miles in advance of where we then were and would hold it unless again compelled to retreat, in which case he would give us timely notice. There were two houses near by—the one nearer us, on the south, and the other just around the point of a ridge, on the north of the pike. We stopped at the one on the south for the night. This house stood a short distance from the road. Just after daylight next morning fighting commenced between the advancing Federals and our cavalry a very short distance in advance of where we were, and almost immediately, but not until I had taken my place between the house and pike, our cavalry dashed by—calling to us to "get out of that," and followed so closely by one of the enemy's cavalrymen that I did not "catch on" until he had turned and started back as fast as he came, and he had passed almost behind the point of the ridge before my Mississippi spoke.

My brother Marion who was near me then called my attention to the fact that Doctor Lang was some distance on his way, followed by most of our men, to the rocky pass through which we came the evening before, and which we had then concluded would be a splendid place to makc a stand. However, between us and that point a small stream with a high bank intersected the pike and some of us made our stand there. Very soon the head of a small detachment of the enemy's infantry appeared around the point of the ridge mentioned, and, from our run bank we gave them a volley that effectually checked their advance, caused their rapid retreat and ended the matter finally. We assembled our force and followed them for some distance, passing the house at which they had left their several wounded cavalrymen on our way. We then proceeded, traveling with a guide, by the way of Gaultown, to our destination, as directed, picking up some rations as we advanced. Our wait on the mountain top was short. General Johnson appeared east of Monterey in due time, but before he did so Milroy was reinforced by the arrival of troops from the direction of Franklin, which our lookout saw from his post, on the march; and Johnson, after a brief skirmish with both musketry and artillery, retired to his camp by the way he had come, and of course we had to follow, but in doing so we had to pass the enemy's pickets. Our presence in their rear had evidently been detected, and their pickets had been redoubled and placed so as to intercept us, but after some skirmishing we, at least, passed them safely and returned to camp without further trouble. I have never seen any historical account of this advance by Johnson, but being there, I know it occurred.

No more gallant soldier-comrade than Major Lang, who was later killed at Winchester, Virginia, ever fought and died for his loved South-land.

About the 20th of April, 1862, General Johnson retired from his position at Shenandoah Mountain and went into camp at West View, some seven or eight miles west of Staunton, Virginia. There nearly all of our company reenlisted for "Three years or the War," and, with the exception of its original officers, rejoined the company, which was then reorganized by the election of the writer as captain, and of O. H. P. Lewis, W. H. Wilson and Dudley Long as first, second and third lieutenants in the order named; and we remained Company F of the Thirty-first Virginia Regiment.

General Milroy's main force, with some detachments advanced toward us, was then at McDowell, and General Johnson with some 3,000 men, followed by General T. J. (Stonewall) Jackson with a somewhat larger force, moved to attack him. On the 7th of May, after some skirmishing by our advance we arrived at Wilson's Tavern near Shaw's fork facing Shaw's Ridge, upon which the enemy, with infantry and artillery had made a stand and were firing upon us—the balls from their cannon passing over or by us with little effect. (I am giving these local names from recollection, but I think correctly as then known).

Under these circumstances we offered to, and did, with the sanction of General Johnson, proceed with our company through the woods on our right to the top of the ridge on the left flank of the enemy, while others advanced more slowly on and near the pike. Our maneuver was effective and the Yankees rapidly retreated, leaving behind them considerable material, some blood but no dead, and we fell in with our advance, followed them for a short distance and went into camp for the night. Johnson had six depleted regiments in his command, and on the morning of the 8th, preceded by four of them and followed by the Twenty-fifth Virginia, we continued our march toward McDowell until the head of our column was halted at a point where a wood road in a slight depression came down from the top of Sitlington's Hill from our left and intersected the pike. As I remember it the northwest point of this hill intersects the pike some little distance east of McDowell, the top of it slightly curving, running thence southeastwardly to a point about opposite to where we had halted, and thence, continuing to curve, southward, thus overlooking McDowell and vicinity. The greater part of this ridge, at that time, was covered with timber. We were halted in the early afternoon, and a short time thereafter considerable firing took place on top of the hill at the head of the wood road, and a little later our four leading regiments marched off in that direction, the Fifty-second Virginia considerably in advance, and we had no trouble in telling, by the increased firing, when it reached the battlefield, nor in, for a like reason, discovering when the others arrived and formed in line of battle to their right, for the whole line then immediately became hotly engaged. Somewhat later our regiment and the Twenty-fifth were also ordered forward. When we arrived, our regiment was placed on the left of the Forty-fourth Virginia, which held the extreme right of our forces, while the Twenty-fifth was placed somewhere to our left. We arrived in time to assist in repulsing the last general assault of the enemy. It was now quite late. General Johnson had been wounded, and General Taliaferro had reached the field with three of Jackson's regiments, and had taken command. In the lull following the repulse, the writer, glancing along the front of the Forty-fourth Virginia, the right of which was upon low ground, discovered, at some distance beyond its extreme right, the enemy advancing through the thick timber on the crest of the curving ridge, at once reported that fact to General

Taliaferro, who happened to be near by, and was ordered by him to face his company to the right, pass in rear of the Forty-fourth, and intercept the enemy, which we did, being followed by all the left wing of our regiment and a part of the Twenty-fifth, as we later learned. Just after we had met and commenced firing upon the advancing enemy, our gallant major, Joseph Chenoweth, overtook us and at first, not understanding the significance of our movement or our authority for making it, and not being able to distinguish friend from foe in the semi-darkness, ordered us to cease firing. He was soon undeceived, and drawing and waving his sword, ordered and led us onward. We went and the battle ended; but at this point two gallant Company F boys, Asa Kelley and William Lemon, were mortally wounded.

This battle was fought almost wholly by General Johnson's force. The gallant General Taliaferro with his three brigades from General Jackson's army did not reach the battle-field until late in the evening, after the hardest part of the fighting was over. Therefore, I am very sure that Milroy had more men on that field of battle, from first to last, than did our generals. I also think that our loss in killed and wounded equaled his. Usually more effective shooting is done up than down hill. We had no artillery in the fight while the enemy had, which was necessarily somewhat favorable to them.

We found and captured near and at McDowell a considerable quantity of war material, among other things some cases of fine Enfield rifles—the first I had ever seen.

We followed the retreating Federal army which had fired the woods as it went, through the resultant smoke, until it had passed by, and taken up a strong position beyond Franklin where it had been reenforced by Fremont. There we left it and returned by the way of McDowell to the Shenandoah Valley; stopping on the way to give thanks for the victory won, and to pray for others yet to be given us.

It was upon this McDowell expedition that I first saw General Stonewall Jackson, which I think was at the

Wilson Tavern above mentioned. His appearance did not strike me as forcibly as did that of General Lee when I first saw him at Valley Mountain. I did not speak to him while on this McDowell trip, and do not know how or when he learned of my connection with his army, but when I called, alone, at his tent near Port Republic in the following June, he recognized and addressed me both by name and title, and, in the conversation which followed, gave me to understand that he had known of me ever since the McDowell fight. He also seemed to know that I was from Randolph County where his sister, Mrs. Arnold, then resided, and inquired very kindly of the well-being of herself and family, showing himself the man as well as the general.

CHAPTER IX

AFTER "COMMISSARY" BANKS & BATTLE OF WINCHESTER

Returning from McDowell, General Jackson, marching his army by Bridgewater—one of the prettiest towns I ever saw—reached New Market, Virginia on the Valley Pike, about May 20, 1862, and near there was joined by General R. S. Ewell's division, and our regiment—Thirty-first Virginia, and the Twenty-fifth Virginia, together with other regiments from Johnson's command—was transferred to said division, of which it became the 4th Brigade, to the command of which Brigadier General Arnold Elza [Elzey] was assigned. General Banks then occupied his fortified position at Strasburg with some 17,000 men—a force about equal to that commanded by General Jackson. A day or two later, led by Ewell's division, our entire army, with the exception of a small force left to face Banks and cover our movement, crossed the Massanutten Mountain and camped in the Luray Valley. Next morning we proceeded to and captured Front Royal with a large amount of commissary stores, and Colonel Kenley's entire First Maryland Federal Cavalry Regiment. Colonel Johnson's First Maryland Confederate Cavalry Regiment, first alone, defeated that of Kenley, and later was principally concerned in its capture. We camped some distance north of Port Republic, and next morning Ewell with part of his division marched for Middletown in rear of Banks at Strasburg. Our brigade followed Jackson. In the mean time Banks had learned of our flank movement and was retreating through Middletown and our advance ran into his column at that place; capturing a long wagon train with an immense amount of commissary stores and war material, together with over 1,000 men and an equal number of horses; and learning that the most of Banks' army had already escaped through Middletown on its way to Winchester, General Jackson immediately followed him, marching, with his advance skirmishing with the rear-guard of the enemy the entire night, and arriving in front of Winchester just at daylight. It had been a toilsome night-march with frequent pauses none of which were long enough to give us a rest. Just as darkness fell we had passed through the little village of Newtown—now Stephens City—where my family had resided for a short time prior to the fall of 1852.

Here my brother Marion and I, after ten years absence, again met our mother's sister, Mrs. Mary Nisewanger, who had lived there for years. Here we again, also, met many of our childhood friends, who, with Aunt Mary, gave us cordial and substantial greeting. Indeed the coming of our whole army was welcomed with the wildest demonstrations of delight by the people of Newtown en masse. They apparently hailed us as deliverers from the insufferable restraint that had been placed upon them by our joint enemies. We also here learned that our dear old aunt was, on account of her many kindnesses to Confederate soldiers, known to nearly all of them, who had been operating in that section, as "Aunt Mary."

The Battle of Winchester between Generals Jackson and Banks opened early on the morning of the 25th of May, and, for a short time, was fiercely contested. Up until this time our regiment had taken no part in any of the fighting since our return from McDowell, and even now it, with the rest of our brigade, was, at the beginning of the battle, held in reserve in its position on the main pike leading into the town; but in a short time we were thrown to the front, arriving in the center of our advanced line on the pike just as General Jackson ordered the general advance of his whole line; and away we went on the double-quick, nor halted until after passing through and some distance beyond the town. The scenes enacted as we passed along its streets beggars description—fully equaling those we had witnessed at Newtown. Regardless of bursting shells, flying bullets and the groans of the wounded, men, women and children thronged the narrow, battle-laden streets; some to cheer us; some to administer to, and comfort as best they could, our wounded, and all to welcome us.

And as we passed onward, the writer saw beautiful young ladies—and Winchester had many such—who had been delicately nurtured, extending helpful hands to our fallen comrades who most needed help. Glorious girls! We then felt, as we yet feel, a great pride in your young womanhood. Here, too, our coming seemed to be welcomed by all of southern sympathies, as deliverers from the intolerably oppressive rule and presence of the Federal authorities. Alas! we had again to leave them all too soon.

Our infantry pursued the enemy northward until arriving in the vicinity of Stephenson's Depot; where, being utterly worn out, we went into camp on and near the Martinsburg Pike. From this point our cavalry continued the pursuit to the Potomac River, but for some reason not known to the writer, gave us but little or no aid upon our advance there from Winchester. If it had, undoubtedly our capture from the enemy both in men and material, large as it was, must have been much greater. It was said at the time, that the apparent inactivity of his cavalry, which was then under the command of the gallant General Ashby, caused a temporary estrangement between that officer and General Jackson; but if so, it passed away before Ashby fell, fiercely fighting near Harrisonburg a few days later; for Jackson's tribute to his life and memory, then tendered, was beautifully appreciative of his character, both as man and soldier.

We remained in this camp for two or three days, and while there, Marion and I visited our nearby home of 1850-1, near where we met, and were welcomed by many youthful friends of the "olden time." Upon leaving this camp we maneuvered for a day or two in the direction of Charles Town and Harpers Ferry, but on account of the approach of Fremont from the west and Shields from the east to Strasburg in our rear, we here received orders to retrace our steps to that place as rapidly as possible and we complied strictly with orders, carrying with us not only all our prisoners, but all the commissary stores and other material taken from the enemy, the capture of which, had given to Banks the appellation of "Jackson's Commissary." As we passed through Winchester and Newtown, the bright smiles that greeted our advance were replaced by scalding tears, making scenes too pathetic to write about or dwell upon. Arriving at Strasburg our command, under Ewell, pushed back and held that of Fremont, on our right, and General Winder did the same with that of Shields on our left, until Jackson with the residue of his army passed through and safely on toward the future battlefields of Cross Keys and Port Republic, to which we followed.

CHAPTER X

BATTLES OF CROSS KEYS AND PORT REPUBLIC

Our whole brigade, including our regiment, took an active part in both of these battles. That of Cross Keys was fought wholly by the division of General Ewell, and under his immediate supervision. The battlefield was undoubtedly well selected, and our troops splendidly handled. General Fremont's army, engaged in that fight, must have doubled our own, but we were so placed and maneuvered that it is possible he thought he was confronted by Jackson's entire army, as claimed, which accounted for his long delay in making his attack.

Our brigade was placed in rear of Ewell's general line of battle, in support of his main battery which occupied a position about the center of the line, having a small infantry force with it. From a hillock near the center of our regiment, we saw the enemy's center and right advance to, and take position on, his intended line of battle; but could not see the left of his line. After taking his position, General Fremont remained inactive, or virtually so, for some time; but about 4 o'clock his left and our right became engaged, and for a time fought furiously. Two of our regiments were sent forward to reenforce their comrades there, and it was not long until we could tell from the firing that the enemy were being driven back. In the mean time the battery in our front was hotly engaged with some of the enemy's but more than held its own, thereby preventing a charge projected by the enemy in its immediate front. The fighting had now extended along our entire left wing, and the residue of our brigade was advanced to support it. Notwithstanding the enemy's repeated charges thereupon, we arrived in time to effectively do so. Just at nightfall the enemy retired and the battle ended. Our loss was very small; that of the enemy much larger. The writer was unhurt but considerably scared, almost scarred, by a closely passing grape-shot. This fight took place June 8.

The battle of Port Republic was altogether different from that of Cross Keys. We retired from our position at the latter, about the middle of the night following our fight there, and arrived in front of the position we were to take at Port Republic on the next morning, June 9, 1862—some time after the commencement of the battle there.

There was no great difference in the number of Federals and Confederates engaged in this battle; but the former occupied a remarkably strong defensive position—almost unassailable from the front. I do not know where the other regiments of our brigade were placed, but we took position about the left center of our whole battle-line. We were on what was then known as the Lewis Farm, and the ground in our front was level and cleared. Just a short distance in advance of where we first took position we could see a large field covered with golden hued wheat, ready for the sickle of the reaper. We were ordered forward, and through a murderous hail of bullets, both from cannon and small arms, to which we replied as best we could, reached, passed through and were halted near the farther side of that trampled field of wheat. While gaining and occupying this position our loss was very heavy. Among others, here our gallant major, Joseph Chenoweth, was killed. Our ardor had carried us too far and we were ordered to retire, which we did to about the middle of the wheat field, where we again fronted the enemy in line of battle, lying down. Our retirement even for so short a distance, was a mistake, for our loss in doing so was fully equal to that incurred in our advance. From our position in the wheat, while lying down at least, we fought with less loss, although the golden heads of wheat, severed from their stems above us by both cannon and rifle balls, showered down upon us. Our stay here was short. Our whole line was now ordered to advance, and with the Confederate yell, that afterward became so celebrated, resounding from its entire length, and possibly to some extent actuated by a desire to revenge our fallen comrades, we rushed forward, sweeping the enemy from, and several miles beyond, the battle-field, with a loss in men greater than we had yet sustained, besides that of much war material. And so the battle of Port Republic, and with it General Jackson's incomparable Valley campaign, ended. For the length of the time engaged, the loss in our regiment was very heavy—probably more so than in any other battle of the war. It reached, in killed and wounded, about fifty percent of those engaged. Two of our company, John Long and James Ruckman, were among the killed.

We thought at the time that, probably, we had been ordered to and through the wheat field mentioned for the purpose of attracting the attention of the enemy, until General Taylor made his right flank attack which contributed so largely to our victory. We think so still.*

This battle occurred on the southeast side of the Shenandoah River, over which we had crossed upon retiring from Cross Keys—burning the bridge behind us; and just as it ended, General Fremont, whom we had repulsed and left at Cross Keys, appeared on the hills on the northwest side thereof, from which he plainly witnessed the discomfiture, hasty retreat and disappearance of the army of his associate, General Shields; carrying with it all his plans and hopes for a successful issue to a campaign from which he, as well as his superiors, expected so much. His helplessness to interfere on account of the intervening deep and turbid river was, probably, the "Unkindest cut of all."*

His disappointment and chagrin were so great that, just after General Shields' army disappeared in the

---

* A similar version of this battle was given to Jedediah Hotchkiss on April 8th, 1863 by Capt. "Hardin" of the 31st Va. [undoubtedly Harding].
* Shakespeare, *Julius Caesar*, III, ii, 188.

distance, his cannon opened upon some of our burying details, one of which was engaged, under the charge of a chaplain, in burying the dead of his own army. It is to be hoped that this was done by mistake, but that it was done for some reason is undeniable; and at the time, perhaps wrongly, we attributed it to Fremont's animosity, aroused by the confronting situation.

Our sensations while lying in Lewis' wheat were not pleasant to any great extent. Our old Tuckahoe friend expressed the situation pretty well when he said that he was lying there badly scared, while the cannon balls were cutting off the wheat heads above him and saying as they passed "Whar-iz-you? Whar-iz-you?' And the writer is wont to tell inquiring friends that, if he has ever made any impression in the world, it will be found in the ground where once stood Lewis' field of wheat.

CHAPTER XI

STONEWALL JACKSON, THE MAN

While falling back from Strasburg after eluding the converging columns of Generals Fremont and Shields, we learned from a source deemed reliable that the Federal authorities, then holding Randolph County, Virginia, from which most of our Company F, Thirty-first Virginia Regiment had enlisted, were compelling some of our parents to leave their homes and go South through their lines.

On the evening of June 6, 1862—the same day General Ashby was killed—three of our company, Eugenius Hutton, Milton Crouch and Noah S. Channell (than whom three more gallant gentlemen or braver soldiers never wore the gray—all of whom shed their blood and two of whom gave their lives as tribute to the cause they loved) came to me and requested that I procure for them, if possible, leave of absence for a few days in order that they might visit our county and learn the facts in relation to the report, and to lend such aid to the refugees as might be in their power. The campaign was still unfinished, and I felt it would be useless to make such application at the time and so informed them; but when the company roll was called that evening none of these boys answered to his name, nor did they appear again during our stay in the Valley. Naturally I was greatly concerned for their safety. On account of the enemy whose lines they had to penetrate, they would necessarily be in great danger. Besides this, the orders against absence without leave were rightly very strict, their violation heavily punished, and if the absentees were caught and forcibly returned, possibly the death penalty might be inflicted.

After the battle of Port Republic, June 9, 1862, which closed the Valley campaign, we went into camp for a few days near that place. General Jackson was with us, occupying a "fly tent." I called at his quarters, found him alone and was invited in. I then told him of the report we had received from home and that many of us had parents and sisters there who must necessarily suffer if compelled to become refugees, making the case as strong as I could and closing by asking permission to send two or three men through the lines to look after and take care of the situation, but did not tell him that they had already gone. He refused my request, sternly and apparently absolutely. I undertook to plead our cause, and convinced myself, at least, that it was a meritorious one, and that my request should be granted; but the General remained unconvinced and firm in his denial and I turned to leave the tent.

Possibly I was irritated, and probably my countenance or bearing indicated it, for just as I reached the opening in the tent General Jackson spoke very sharply and sternly, I thought, saying, "Stop, Captain. What are you going to do?" My reply, in effect, was that I intended to assume the responsibility of sending two or three reliable men through the lines to ascertain the facts in the case and to provide for the situation as far as possible, and that I would be found at my quarters when wanted, to account for my action. A flash as of a glint of tempered steel shot from the General's eyes and lighted up his countenance, but he bowed his head upon his hands as he was sitting in his camp chair or stool, and I could see that he was strangely agitated, and [I] stood still for what seemed then to me to be an almost interminable interval of time, but which in fact was but for a few moments, and then he lifted his head. The transition in the whole man was wonderful. His countenance was bright and beautiful—his voice low and sweet and full of pathos as he said, "Well, Captain, it is a hard case. I fully appreciate and sympathize with your feelings and you can do as you please."

It is possible that I do not remember his exact words—I think I do, but there was no mistaking, as there will be no forgetting, the kindness of the heart that prompted them, and the only condition attached to his permission was that I let him know, when the boys came back, the result of their investigation. I did so when they returned to us at Ashland just before the Seven Days' fight at Richmond, and the fact that the report we had heard was only true to a very limited extent, seemed to give to him as much pleasure as it did to us. General Jackson never learned of my deception.

CHAPTER XII

SEVEN DAYS' BATTLE NEAR RICHMOND
BATTLE OF GAINES' MILL

So many variant claims about and descriptions of this battle have been made and given by others, that the writer here attempts to describe that part of it which fell under his immediate observation with some degree of hesitancy, although his recollection of that part is very vivid.

Our command bivouacked at and near Hundley's Corner on the night of the 26th of June, 1862. Our march that day had been somewhat retarded by blockaded roads and detachments of Federal soldiers, and we had heard heavy cannonading, which had continued until night-fall, in the direction of Mechanicsville. On the next morning we resumed our march, still impeded as on the day before, and still hearing cannonading, intermingled as we progressed with the rattle of small arms, on our right. When we first started we apparently inclined to the left, and while entangled in the intervening blockades across the roads, General D. H. Hill's division, from Lee's army, passed across our front, and, bearing a little to the left of the line we were taking, marched on. We continued on our course for some distance and then turned, somewhat abruptly, and marched almost directly toward the sound of the battle that had for some time been waging on our right. When we arrived near that battle-ground, General Elza [Elzey], with most of our brigade, which he still commanded, was placed to the left of the road running east from Gaines' house, at the brow of a considerable elevation when coming from the west, as we had.

Here we were formed in the edge of the woods, behind an old rail-fence, with our right resting on the road. In our immediate front was an extensive plateau, slightly descending, and dotted with a scattering growth of stunted pine which reached to within a distance of about two hundred yards from our line, thus leaving a nearly cleared space of that width between. Our position was excellent, and, for some time we held it with but little fighting. In the meantime our troops, both to the left and right of us, were more heavily engaged. At times our line on our right seemed to recede, but only to advance again almost immediately. About 5 o'clock our turn came, and we were furiously attacked. The first Federals that reached our side of the growth of pine mentioned, were dressed partly in red. They came no farther. Nor did any of them or any of their comrades in any charge later made on that fateful evening, and they made several, succeed in advancing beyond the line where the men in red were first stopped. We maintained our position, with but little loss, throughout the battle; expending nearly all our ammunition. J. R. Apperson and the writer who stood by his side, each fired over forty rounds, and both were slightly wounded—not sufficiently so to be a cause of pride, or a reason for leaving the firing line. While this fight was on, I heard my comrade, David Shelton, inhale the smoke-laden air so loudly that I turned to see what was the matter. He had been shot through the fleshy part of his left hand between the thumb and fore-finger. There was a stream of water a short distance to our rear and I directed him to go there and leave his hand in it. He said, "All right, Captain, but my gun is loaded and I will take another crack before I go" and he did.

Shortly before the battle closed, General Elza, who was standing near by, facing the enemy, was struck by a rifle ball which entered near his mouth and apparently passed through the lower part of his head. We thought he was dead when we reached him, and so left him, but he lived until some time after the war closed. All that part of our brigade, including our regiment, which occupied the position mentioned, took an active part in the general charge made late in the evening, which swept the enemy with heavy loss in men and material, in confusion from the field, and ended the long drawn-out struggle by a complete victory.

Weary and foot-sore, but elated, we rested that night, amid some of the trophies of our victory, on the road near Grapevine bridge.

This divested of all exaggeration is all I know of this fight; but of Federal General Carman's description of it, when not so divested, as it appears in the Americana—a standard encyclopedia, I desire to speak.

He says, in effect, that General Porter, with but little over 20,000 men faced General Lee with 57,000 men from as early as 2 o'clock until about 5 o'clock, on the afternoon of June 27.

As given by our best informed authorities General Lee's entire fighting force, after he had been joined by Jackson, did not, at most, exceed 75,000 men. Of that number he had left about 30,000 facing General McClellan's left wing south of the river; thus leaving him for this battle on the north side of the river a scattered force of men, which, when concentrated, would aggregate only about 45,000.

General Jackson with his own corps, the division of Whiting and the division of D. H. Hill, did not reach Lee's line of battle until about 5 o'clock on the afternoon of June 27, and, as the writer remembers it, on account of the time taken in distributing and placing these forces on that line, most of them did not become actively engaged until a short time after that hour. Therefore it seems safe to say that up until 5 o'clock at least, General Lee fought General Porter, no matter what force the latter had under him, with less than 30,000 men, instead of 57,000 as claimed by Carman. While we do not know the actual number of men General Porter had under him in this fight, we do know that General McClellan, said that he then had at Richmond an effective force of 112,000 men, which would have given him, at least, 105,000 fighting men with which to meet General Lee; and it would be passing strange—indeed quite unbelievable—that he would have let his lieutenant fight a superior force of the enemy, for a day and a half, without reinforcing him; and we do not believe he did. We further know that among the Federals we captured that evening, some were from Porter's, some from Franklin's and some from Sumner's corps, and all looked as if they had been fighting the greater part of the day. We do not know from whence Carman derived his information as to the number of men Porter commanded in this fight. We have never seen it so given by any other writer.

We notice that Carman does not here mention the fact that several Federal batteries were planted on the south side of the river at the mouth of Powhite Creek so as to sweep the ground in front of Porter's main works on the north side, and which gave him more effectual aid than any division he had with him.

CHAPTER XIII

SEVEN DAYS' FIGHT NEAR RICHMOND
MALVERN HILL

On the morning of June 28, General Ewell, with our division, left the Gaines' Mill battle field and marched down on the north side of the Chickahominy River to Dispatch Station on the York River Railroad. The station had been fired either by General Stuart or the enemy before we arrived. We proceeded to tear up the railroad toward the river and to guard or destroy the bridge thereover. Far away to the south we could see the enemy. While watching them we first heard, and then saw, in the distance, a detached locomotive coming on with ever increasing speed until it arrived within about half a mile of us, when it apparently exploded, somersaulted and left the track with such a tremendous shock that the earth and air trembled and quivered until the twigs and bark from the trees above, showered down upon us, causing a regular stampede among affrighted men and horses; and a temporary deafness to all. Later some of us walked over to examine the wreck. We found that the Yankees had loaded upon, and firmly attached to, that locomotive the largest cannon we had ever seen; and we supposed they had charged it to the muzzle, cut the fuse so as to discharge it among us, opened the throttle to the engine and let it go. If our conjecture as to their motive was right, it was only defeated by the rapidity with which the thing came at us; and they well nigh accomplished their object, by the shock and scare they gave us, even as it was. Before we had fully recovered from this shock, we saw huge columns of smoke arising from McClellan's principal depot of supplies at White House, which had been fired by the enemy, but General Stuart got there in time to save part of the supplies.

54

On the morning of the 29th we went further down the river and guarded Deep Bottom Bridge until late that evening when we were ordered to return to Grapevine Bridge, cross the river there and follow the rest of Jackson's command which had joined in the pursuit after General McClellan, and we did as ordered. We here met Brigadier General Jubal A. Early, who took command of our brigade in the place of the wounded General Elza. That was my first glimpse of General Early. We did not overtake General Jackson in time to engage—at least we were not called upon to engage—in any battle, to any considerable extent, until we arrived at Malvern Hill, on the afternoon of July 1. We were weary with our long march down and back on the north side of the river, and were now held in reserve until late in the evening. Our position, however, was in range of the enemy's numerous batteries planted on the summit of Malvern Hill, and many cannon balls and shells passed by us or over us. Generals Lee and Jackson had taken positions near us, had dismounted, were facing each other, and each had his horse's bridle rein in his hand or looped over his arm. It was nearly sundown when we were ordered forward. We passed within a few feet of the Generals, and just as our company was marching by them, a shell went over us, low down, apparently passing directly over them, and bursting immediately over us. Its velocity threw most of the fragments beyond us and they were buried in the ground nearby, but some of them struck among us, killing our comrade J. Quick and wounding others. I have been thus minute in giving this incident because I have read after some writer who said that a bomb-shell had exploded between these Generals while talking on this battle field, and I have thought that, perhaps, the incident here given furnished the foundation for this.

Amidst the thunder of cannon resounding from the summit of this hill, and from the enemy's gunboats on the James River, we pressed forward to the front, passing many dead on our way, and leaving some of our own, whose march had ended. There had been a lull in the rifle firing when we started, but soon it began again, lending its treble to the harsher sound of the cannon. Our own loss was not great, but seeming destruction hovered over and around us and apparently awaited our coming farther on. The writer was not wounded himself, but was sprinkled with the blood of others who were. With but little actual fighting we at last reached our appointed place, just at dark, taking position not over two hundred yards—less I think—from the batteries on the hill that had been shelling us, and which kept up their firing until about 10 o'clock at night, when they ceased and the fight was over. The enemy then had no unwounded men between us and their artillery. Our names were listed by our adjutant, by order of General Early, and we remained in that position throughout the night, during which the enemy retreated, leaving their unburied dead, many of their wounded and great quantities of quartermaster stores and other war material behind them. Brother Marion was one of the first—probably the first—picket to discover that they had vacated their position. Their retreat had evidently been commenced early in the night when the noise would not attract our attention. Our command advanced at once, and followed, with but little skirmishing, until we neared Harrison's Landing where they had sought the protection of their gunboats and fortifications.

As we advanced, evidences of their hasty retreat and disorganization were seen on every hand and all along our way. Indeed their army apparently scattered and retreated upon different roads and paths and through fields, leaving equipment everywhere. We remained in front of Harrison's Landing for about a week, then returned to Richmond, remained there a few days, and started for Gordonsville, Banks and Pope; the latter of whom we understand had his headquarters in the saddle, from which he always looked forward, never rearward.

I believe that General Lee said that, under ordinary circumstances, McClellan's army should have been destroyed at Richmond. Why I do not know. Carman in his description of the Seven Days' Battles says that its destruction was prevented by, "The skill of McClellan in conducting the retreat, but more to the fighting qualities of his subordinate officers and men," and again we do not understand why. It will be conceded, we think, that McClellan had, in men, at least, 4 to Lee's 3; that his equipment outranked Lee's 3 to 1, and that his defensive fighting, especially from his entrenched positions at Gaines' Mill and prior thereto, was, at least, 2 to 1 in his favor. Then why not attribute Lee's failure to destroy his army to these facts, instead of the far-fetched and absurd reasons given by Carman? The greater wonder is that McClellan retreated at all, or that Lee could compel him to do so.

Ridpath in his General History says that "McClellan was clearly victorious at Malvern Hill"; that in the judgment of after times he "might have made a successful advance on Richmond"; that "Lee's army was shattered"; and that McClellan's army of superior numbers "was ready and able to continue the struggle." This misinformation was evidently, if at all, derived from someone who was not on the ground at the time. It is a fact that General Lee's advanced line was temporarily repulsed at Malvern Hill, but his main army immediately moved forward and took position within two hundred yards of where the enemy's cannon that had repulsed it stood on the hill crest, and remained there throughout the coming night, able, willing and anxious to continue the conflict in the dawn of the morrow; and with its morale wholly unimpaired. On the other hand, the fact that the enemy, in the night-time, retreated from the battle-field without burying their dead, or caring for or removing their wounded, with many other evidences of their hasty and disorganized flight, gave irrefragable proof of the demoralized condition of the morale of their army; nor can this condition of things be charged to the timidity or hesitancy of General McClellan. An order to retreat does not contemplate a disorderly rout. Certainly the "Judgment of after times," or Mr. Ridpath, was here at fault. And, being there, we speak whereof we know.

George Harding
Eldest brother of French
(1835-1862)

CHAPTER XIV

BATTLE OF CEDAR MOUNTAIN

We reached Gordonsville and went into camp there about the 20th of July. On account of the fighting Yankees, hot weather, meager rations and impure water which had been our portion on the Chickahominy River, we were somewhat run down and emaciated when we arrived there. However, rest, with the change for purer air and water and better rations, soon recuperated us. Blackberries were in season and plentiful. The way we lived and thrived on blackberry dumplings was astonishing; and by the end of the two weeks we remained in this camp, we had gained our normal condition and were ready for whatever the future held for us. While here our brother, George, joined us. He was physically unfit for military service, but had been, for personal reasons, reported as disloyal, to the Federal authorities, by a troublesome neighbor, and was compelled to leave home or suffer arrest. He had left the rest of our family well but was himself quite ill and feeble, so much so that his condition gave but little promise for his future.

Our army was now not only in good spirits and physical condition, but had armed itself, from the battle-fields of the Valley and the Seven Days' Fight on the Chickahominy, especially with small arms; much better than had formerly been the case. The writer, who always carried a gun, had become possessed of a splendid short Enfield rifle, and many of his comrades were so armed.

We marched from this camp to Cedar mountain, where on August 9, 1862, under Stonewall Jackson, we fought the bloody battle of Cedar Mountain. General Banks commanded the Federal army.

Our regiment was placed at some distance in advance of our regular battle line with orders to hold our position as long as possible.

It was very warm both by reason of the heat of the sun and because of the flying bullets. However, we held our position and repulsed the enemy until they flanked us and commenced pouring volleys into our left and rear, when we were ordered back to position on our main line. Just then our color bearer, Marks, who was one of my personal friends, was killed by my side, and though unable to speak he gave me a look as he fell, or rather as I caught and laid him down, that I never can forget. Almost at the same moment, before some of us had started back, my gallant comrade, life-long friend and former schoolmate, Lieutenant O. H. Perry Lewis fell severely—we thought at the time mortally—wounded almost in reach of me. We succeeded in having him carried safely behind our regular battle line, but in doing so his brother John—another special friend of mine—and myself were thrown considerably in rear of the rest of our command and remained there for the protection, to some extent, of our wounded comrade and the stretcher bearers who were carrying him. The temporarily victorious enemy advanced upon us rapidly, and we did what we could to retard them, keeping our position in the rear until our comrades were safe within our lines; and [we] were slowly following, side by side, almost spent with heat and exertion, when the "leaden messenger of death" also overtook John and pierced his faithful heart, and he, too, looked up at me and fell dying, but with a bright smile lingering on his boyish face, and without requiem, other than that sung by the whistling of bullets and the thunder of cannon. When I stooped to raise him, he was dead.

Among all the gallant boys who fought and died in battle for the South-land—and there were many—there fell none truer, braver or nobler than he. Composing his body as best I could, alone I proceeded to our battle line, where our company, almost completely exhausted, rested.

My immediate later action is to me now inexplicable. Probably I then had no reason for it, other than the knowledge that some of my comrades had been left dead, and others wounded, on the battle field. Be that as it may, one of the color guard—Martin Mulvey—had brought off our regimental flag; which I at once caught up and waved, called on the boys to follow me, and, without orders, started back to meet the enemy. Those men never failed to respond to such a call, no matter what their condition if able to walk, nor did they then, but answered with a ringing cheer, and back we went in a slightly broken line composed not only of our regiment but of the entire division, with our flag at the most advanced point in the line; and kept on going, shooting and cheering until we had swept the enemy from the field, and the victory was won.

We did not know at the time that our action was specially noticed by our commanding officers; and I supposed that if it were, I would be censured for it; but soon after we had been ordered to halt, Major Hale, acting as aide to General Ewell, rode up to where we were lying down, resting, and, in the name of General Ewell, suggested that the latter be authorized to recommend me for promotion to a colonelcy.

No vacancy existed in our regiment at the time, and the acceptance of such promotion would necessarily remove me from it to serve elsewhere. No one was more surprised by the offer than myself, and before I could answer, my company comrades, who had heard it, surrounded [me] and begged me not to accept it and leave them; and I chose to remain with them; thus sacrificing my ambition on the alter of my friendship.

CHAPTER XV

*CAMPAIGN AGAINST GENERAL POPE--
ON THE RAPIDAN AND RAPPAHANNOCK*

We returned from Cedar Mountain to the vicinity of Gordonsville, and about the middle of August moved forward to Mount Pisgah, near the Rapidan, where we camped for a few days and guarded the fords across that river, while the enemy were guarding their fords from the opposite side; and we sometimes talked to and traded commodities with, and at other times shot at, them thereacross [sic]—more frequently shooting. We here first learned that on certain days when atmospheric conditions were favorable, and we had a ditch in which to stand and drop to shield ourselves, we could by watching the smoke coming from a rifle muzzle dodge its bullet, even when shot from the short distance of less than one hundred and fifty yards; and while we occasionally made use of such knowledge, in order to draw the enemy's fire so our men could more safely rise and return it, we further learned that there was considerable danger in doing so. We also here learned that the writer had made no mistake in the selection of his Enfield rifle and, generally, that blackberry cobblers were the greatest institutions that ever blessed a soldier's life.

After remaining here a few days, General Lee with the rest of the army arrived, and we moved forward, crossing the Rapidan at Somerville Ford, reaching the Rappahannock near Beverly's Ford, and going up the south side of that river to the vicinity of Warrenton Springs; keeping near the river all the way, and while doing so, suffering considerable loss from the enemy's batteries planted at many points on the opposite side. Our lieutenant, W. H. Wilson was struck on the temple with a fragment of shell. I was walking near him at the time, heard the sound of the blow, and turned and caught him as he fell. He seemed shocked and dizzy, but otherwise not badly hurt and talked to me so rationally that I seated him on a log and marched on thinking he would soon be able to follow and knowing he would do so as soon as able; but we later learned that he did not come to himself for several hours, and would be unable for duty several weeks. We do not know why we were marched so close to the river; probably we were looking for a ford at which to cross.

The bridge near Warrenton Springs where we halted had been destroyed, but there appeared to be no organized force of the enemy on the opposite shore, and our brigade, aided by an old near-by mill dam, crossed over the river, and, with but little opposition, took possession of the Springs. Almost immediately thereafter, rain commenced and continued to fall, very heavily, until the river was so swollen that we were as completely isolated from the rest of our army, except as to the slight protection its artillery might afford us, as though it did not exist; thus leaving our brigade to confront Pope's entire army. Unquestionably we were not only badly scared but had good reason to be. However, General Early was equal to the occasion. He formed us partly in the woods and partly upon uneven ground, in the best manner possible to conceal the smallness of his force, and at the same time boldly advanced a long line of skirmishers indicative of a large army.

The writer was on that skirmish line all of the 23rd day of August and part of the following night, watching., and doing what he could to retard the cautious advance of the enemy. General Early visited us several times during the day, was certainly anxious, but apparently cheerful. While he knew of us at Malvern Hill, Cedar Mountain, and on the Rapidan; yet it was here that we first had any considerable conversation with him. We found him to be a gallant, genial gentleman. We also found that while humorously inclined, he was prompt and stern in his movements, and commands, to meet the threatened danger.

Our skirmish line slowly receded before the enemy's until dark, then held its position so close to them that we could hear them talking. We retired about midnight, fell in the rear and returned to the south side of the river over a skeleton bridge hastily prepared for the purpose; and on the morning of the 24th, much relieved, rejoined the rest of our army.

We here found brother George, who appeared to be in worse condition than when he first joined us. He seemed to be suffering from a slight attack of fever; and we sought and found a private family that agreed to take care of him, and leaving him there with some means and two of our comrades, who were also on sick leave, to assist in caring for him, we returned to our company. Next morning, August 25, we started on our famous flank march for Manassas Junction in [the] rear of General Pope's army, going by the way of Salem and Thoroughfare Gap; sometimes marching in the roads and sometimes by short cuts through the fields. On the day we started we breakfasted on abbreviated rations, dined on half rations of unripe corn and fried green apples, and supped about midnight on half rations of fried green apples and unripe corn. Next day we breakfasted on what we had left over from supper the night before, dined on a tightened cartridge box belt and reached Bristoe Station and a reasonably good supper, furnished by the Yankees, that evening.

The next morning the main body of our army moved on and joined General Stuart at Manassas; leaving our division, under General Ewell, at Bristoe to retard the advance of Pope's army which was retiring from the Rappahannock, and moving upon us. It arrived some time in the afternoon; and was immediately attacked and driven back by our division, and although speedily reinforced, we held it in check for some time, then retired, unpursued, I think, and reached Manassas late that evening. Here we found abundant rations, which had also been furnished by the Yankees, awaiting us, and near here we remained for the most of the night, spending the greater part of it in filling up.

Many of our men made this march entirely barefooted, and many others practically so.

CHAPTER XVI

CAMPAIGN AGAINST GENERAL POPE
GROVETON OR GAINESVILLE

This battle, fought on the 28th of August, 1862, is historically known by both these names. At the time we called it Groveton. It was really the beginning of the second Battle of Manassas.

When we arrived at the Junction late on the evening of the 27th, while we found an immense amount of commissary stores there, we discovered that the best eatables had been appropriated by those who had preceded us. However, we were glad to take part of what was left; and receiving orders to supply ourselves with three days' rations, proceeded to comply, as best we could, before leaving next morning. It was a big job; not so much on account of the amount of provision, such as it was, on hand, as on account of our inability to carry the necessary quantity. On the 28th we wandered around in the vicinity of the first Manassas battle-ground until late in the afternoon. All our actions on that day were apparently for the purpose of misleading the Yankees as to where we were and would be, and of getting away with three days' rations in one, and we were eminently successful along both lines. Late in the evening we heard Longstreet's cannon at Thoroughfare Gap. The sound was very welcome for it gave promise that he and General Lee would be with us on the morrow; and our corps had been and still was critically isolated from them.

About the same time we heard Longstreet's guns, a column of the enemy was passing near us on the Warrenton road, and General Jackson, apparently no longer desiring to conceal his movements or position, ordered General Ewell with his own and Taliaferro's division to attack it. He at once did so and a terrific battle resulted. On account of our rear-guard fighting on the 27th our brigade was still in the rear, and was not ordered forward until near nightfall. Just before arriving at the front, we appeared to pass over a plat of slightly elevated ground. Here a perfect hail of rifle bullets met and swept by and over us. It probably, indeed it must have, appeared to us more frightful than it really was, but it did not so impress us at the time, and I feel sure that, at least some of us, felt like making a precipitate retreat, and doubtless would have done so but for the onlooking eyes of our braver comrades. The writer then thought and yet thinks that he felt both the wind and the heat caused by the passing bullets; and certain it is that something caused my head and hat to part company. I attributed it to the bullets, but some of the boys claimed it resulted from involuntary dodging. Maybe so, but how could they see in the dark? However this may be, apparently as much danger lurked behind as before us, and we went forward until we reached our comrades on the firing line where they were lying down and we took our places beside them. The distance between our line and that of the enemy was very short. The ground upon which we were lying quivered with every discharge of cannon on either line, and the space between was alight with flames spitting from gun and rifle both large and small. Taken all together it was one of the most uncomfortable positions that the writer or his command ever occupied, and I think we all so considered it, and now after the passage of the many intervening years, so look back upon it. However, it did not last. Almost immediately after our arrival the enemy retreated. Whether they did so because of the added weight or rapidity of our firing, or whether they had about enough of it when we came, I do not know, but I do know that they were gallant soldiers, and that it had been a veritable case of "Greek meeting Greek."

Here the loss on both sides was very heavy. Generals Ewell and Taliaferro were both wounded—the former losing his leg.

CHAPTER XVII

CAMPAIGN AGAINST GENERAL POPE
SECOND BATTLE OF MANASSAS

Early on the morning of the 29th, General Jackson, still facing General Pope's army with his single corps, took position with his right resting near Groveton. Our command was moved to the left. My position while marching was immediately in rear of our color bearer who was carrying his flag-staff at such an angle on his shoulder that the pendant flag hung but a few inches from my face. While the flag was in this position, a cannon ball from the enemy's battery struck and passed through it. It must have been a solid shot for I do not remember hearing any noise other than that caused by the blow and the wind from the passing ball. In any event, it would have knocked me flat if I had not dropped my gun and caught on my hands and knees. Some of the boys ran to my assistance, but when they saw I was still able to help myself, claimed that it was the quickest dodge they had ever seen, that it was the first time they ever saw me on my knees, and that they thought it would be well for me to assume that position oftener in the future than had been my habit in the past. Well-meant badinage that I was too sick to enjoy at the time, but later highly appreciated.

While still marching toward the position we were to occupy, from whence came the sound of desperate fighting, our comrade, Joe Stipe—a very gallant soldier—privately told me that he had a presentiment that he would be killed if he went into the battle, and asked that he be excused from doing so. After a short talk with him, I concluded that he really felt just as he claimed, but answered by calling his attention to the fact that the rest of us were going into the fight which was then raging nearby, that the chances were that many of us would be killed, but that if he thought it was right for him to remain behind he could do so, and so left him. Our battle-line in our immediate front had been formed behind a deep cut in an unfinished railroad, and just then we could tell by the firing that it was falling back, and we were double-quicked forward to support it, found it slowly retiring before over-whelming numbers, still fighting, raised the Confederate yell and charged more rapidly. As we did so, I saw comrade Stipe—Glorious boy!—side by side with our foremost. He fought through that battle, unhurt, but later fell in the battle of the Wilderness.

Our charge was successful, and we swept the enemy back to, out of and some distance beyond said railroad cut, capturing many prisoners, especially in the cut, on our way. From here we were recalled and formed in line of battle on our side of the cut, which was too deep to be occupied as a trench. From this position we fought throughout the remainder of the afternoon; repulsing several successive and desperate charges made by the enemy, with heavy loss to them and some to ourselves. The writer does not remember just how many of these charges were made and repulsed; but he does remember that himself and comrades had apparently spent the longest and most strenuous twenty-four hours of their lives since reaching Groveton on the previous evening; had just passed through an anxious afternoon during every moment of which danger and death stalked beside us; that our ammunition was now well nigh expended—that of some of us entirely so; that we were very weary; that the sun appeared to sink to rest beyond and behind the western hills more slowly than was his wont; and that we longingly awaited the coming of Longstreet or night. We had not long to wait. Soon after we had repulsed the last charge made by the enemy, Longstreet came and we could see his troops taking position on a line running from the right of ours, with his right thrown forward thus making an obtuse angle at their junction; and we thought that the evolutions of those troops as they swung into line was one of the most beautiful and welcomed exhibitions we had ever seen; and thereupon, after a vociferously hearty greeting, we rested; and as night and quiet came, and with them the zephyrs' whispered lullaby of "This is War," we slept. We were very tired.

On the night of the 29th we slept in our places on the day's battle line, ready to renew the struggle on the morning of the 30th, but the forenoon of that day was spent, by both armies, in maneuvering and occasional artillery firing. The position of Lee's army was excellent. General Pope with his greatly superior numbers seemed to hesitate to attack. Once that morning the latter, undoubtedly, undertook to draw the former after him by a feigned retreat. Lee did not go, and Pope advanced to the attack about 2 o'clock in the afternoon. He had a numerous and gallant army, still full of fight, and from that hour until sunset fought, and fought well, as we could abundantly testify when night came. Their first and continued effort seemed to be to break through Jackson's men, so reduced in numbers, and so extended, that they were now formed, without support, in single line of battle. Time and again they threw themselves in dense masses against that line, only to be hurled back decimated, broken and bleeding. The fighting, at times, was close and desperate, and bayonets as well as guns were used, but our line held. As on the preceding day, General Jackson, rode along it several times while the fight was raging, apparently not half so concerned about his personal risk as were we. He had his "War-look" on, but smiled as we cheered him, which we frequently did. His presence unquestionably helped us to hold that line. Someone said it was worth 10,000 men on any battle field. It was there.

Again Longstreet seemed slow in rendering us assistance by attacking the enemy's left, and it was getting late before his advance began to relieve the pressure upon us. We had just repulsed an attack on our front by the enemy—I think it was the last they made that evening—and lay down facing them. Looking round to see what caused such continued cheering, we saw General Jackson quietly riding along in rear of our line. Just then the enemy recommenced shelling us from unseen batteries, and we turned again to face them. I have no distinct recollection of what immediately followed, but I awoke next morning among my comrades, about a mile in advance of where we had been fighting, with a bad headache and a dim recollection of wandering around, aimlessly, with brother Marion the night before. I learned that a fragment of shell had passed so close to my head that my nearby comrades thought from the sound it made that it had hit me. Here life and tragedy stalked so nearly hand in hand and so closely together, that no room for humor was left between, and the boys contented themselves, a little later, by occasionally referring to the alleged fact that my head was hard enough to be bomb-proof.

We had bivouacked on the outskirts of the field of battle where the enemy had fought, and details of our men spent most of the forenoon in caring for their wounded and burying their dead. It was Sunday.

Later in the day, but while still there, one of our comrades, whom we had left with brother George, came and brought us the sad tidings of his sudden and untimely death. He had died on the early morning of the 30th, and our only consolation came from knowing that he had been well and kindly taken care of by his comrades and the good people with whom we had left him at the last; and that he would sleep in a rude coffin and in a marked grave. He had been an enforced wanderer from home and loved ones, and while brother Marion and I were still left to each other, the pathos of the situation was, and is, indescribable.

He was our elder brother and very dear to us. After the close of the war, loving old father and mother went, in a wagon and brought his remains home, and they all now peacefully rest and sleep, side by side, in the old Phares graveyard near Gilman in this [Randolph] county.

I do not remember just where we camped that night but have a distinct recollection of some of the occurrences of the next day and will now write of them.

Joseph (1803-77) & Alice Elliott Harding(1810-84)
Parents of George, Marion, and French Harding

CHAPTER XVIII

CAMPAIGN AGAINST GENERAL POPE
OX HILL, GERMANTOWN, OR CHANTILLY

Although variously named, this battle was actually fought on Ox Hill late on the afternoon of September 1, 1862. While taking our position on the battle-front in the timber on top of the hill, a tremendous rain storm, with but little notice of its coming, burst upon us, and the lowering clouds from which it fell enveloped us in deepest gloom. At that time no enemy appeared in our immediate front, although there was firing both to the right and left of us. The rain and darkness soon passed away, and rifle balls, apparently shot from quite a distance in the woods before us, commenced occasionally to fall among or to pass over us. Just then a one-armed Federal general rode toward us out of the woods, coming on until within a short distance of our line, and directly in front of the left center of Company E of our Thirty-first Regiment, standing immediately on our right in our line of battle. Here he made a momentary pause, apparently discovered his mistake as to who and where we were, and then rapidly turned and started back. We knew that he had unwittingly placed his life in danger and tried to save him by ordering our men not to shoot. If heard by all, it was disobeyed by some, for a few shots were fired by Company E men, and he fell. I have seen General Kearney's [sic] death otherwise described, but unless there were two one-armed Federal generals killed in this fight, this was undoubtedly he. Am glad I tried to save him.

These events succeeded each other almost without pause, soon the rifle firing from the woods in our front rapidly increased, and we could, for the first time that evening, see the advancing enemy. The writer had not, for want of a mark, yet discharged his Enfield, nor did he then. Upon seeing the enemy, I partially raised my gun to fire, advancing my left side and extending my left arm. Just then something stopped me. At first I had a vague impression that I heard something strike my brother who stood next to me on the left. I felt no pain whatever, and my arm remained extended with my gun in my hand until Marion released it from my grasp, and called my attention to the rents in my clothing which marked the passage of the bullet that struck me. Even then I thought I must be but slightly wounded, and so said when it was first suggested that I leave the field. Our good old Doctor Bland later said that my condition resulted from suspended animation caused by the shock given me by the blow of the swiftly coming bullet. Probably so, but if so, short-lived; reanimation at once commenced, and soon thereafter the world and all it contained seemed to be growing dim and distant. However, I kept my feet and with Marion's assistance walked rearward. Just as we did so the setting sun broke through the clouds and shone out brightly low down in the west; and while we were still in range of the enemy's rifle bullets we saw General Jackson, alone and apparently deep in thought, riding toward our battle-line. Upon seeing us he turned and came to meet us. His tone and manner as he inquired about my wound was full of solicitude and kindness, and, as he rode away, he directed my brother to take me to the hospital in the rear, stay with and take good care of me. Kind words the memory of which I still cherish as a precious souvenir—they were the last he ever spoke directly to me.

We reached our field hospital next morning. The doctors, insisting that I was dangerously wounded, were apparently more anxious about my shattered arm than about the wound high up in my side, and concluded that amputation of my arm was necessary. I refused to allow it to be done, and shortly afterward hearing a light step behind me turned and discovered Dr. Bland moving toward me with a handkerchief saturated with chloroform in his hands. Some unpleasant words followed and I walked away through the forest. Two or three days later I apparently awoke from a troubled dream, and found myself in a small building, with cold water dripping from above on my wounds, and Doctor Bland and Brother talking in subdued tones by my side and binding up my broken arm. I lay quiet long enough to hear the doctor tell Marion that on account of the inflammation caused by the wound, my case was now almost hopeless—intimating that if I had allowed him to amputate my arm it would probably have been otherwise. That cold water felt wonderfully pleasant to my heated flesh. I dropped into a natural sleep, and in less than a week was on my feet again. The last time the Doctor visited us at that place, he handed each of us a properly executed sixty day furlough, and next morning we started for the Shenandoah Valley. Traveling very slowly and stopping often on the way, we crossed the Blue Ridge to the home of our Aunt in Newtown. Here we were kindly welcomed and cared for; and remained until I was able to move on without trouble from my wound; and then started homeward.

To further justify my historical skepticism, I desire here to call attention to four inaccurate statements made by Mr. Ridpath in one column of his General History, in reference to General Pope's campaign.

FIRST: — He says that Banks fought the battle of Cedar Run, while attempting to join Pope; while the fact is that Banks then commanded the advance of Pope's army and was sent forward to that field by the latter, who reinforced and joined him near there.

SECOND: — He says that Pope with great audacity threw his army between the forces of Lee and Jackson; while the fact is that Jackson left Lee at Warrenton, marched around Pope's army and took position in his rear, near Bristow and Manassas; thus placing Pope between them, without any aid from him; and his audacity did not even lend him to throw his army between them at Thoroughfare Gap, which he might have done by the exercise of a small portion of it. His effort seemed rather to be to place himself between Jackson and the fortifications at Washington.

THIRD: — From his account thereof, it would appear that the second battle of Manassas was fought on the 28th and 29th of August, and ended indecisively, while the fact is that on those days, Jackson's corps almost wholly alone, was engaged by Pope's army, and that the actual battle of Second Manassas was fought on August 30th, when Lee's army was all engaged, and ended in a decisive victory for Jackson.

FOURTH: — He says that on August 31, Lee's army bore down on the enemy at Chantilly, fought all day and won a victory, while the fact is that only Jackson's men were here engaged and the battle did not occur until the afternoon of September 1st.

CHAPTER XIX

HOME—WOUNDED—SEPTEMBER, 1862
[MARION'S DEATH]

For some reason I have but an indistinct recollection of our movements and of what occurred on this trip while on our way home. I remember that brother Marion went with me; that we rode from Newtown to Staunton on a vehicle of some kind; that I became very sick on the way, and that we took breakfast near McDowell; but I remember nothing else until after we had reached home and were breaking the sad news of brother George's untimely death to our assembled family. The suddenness and sadness of such tidings to a loving old father and mother and affectionate sisters were heart-breaking both to give and receive—almost beyond what kindly human nature could endure. But George was a good boy who had lived a Christian life and died as Christians die; and, all these loved ones he left behind were following in his foot-steps and were living as he had lived; and, therefore, did not mourn his temporary loss as those who have no hope for the future and see no silver lining to the lowering sky hovering over it; but drew consolation from a realization of the certain truth that he had only gone on before, and was awaiting them in that haven of rest to which they would later come where all broken family ties could, and as between them and him, would, be eternally reunited. The writer's sense of loss was imbittered by the knowledge that the man whose act had made brother George a wanderer from home still lived. That man and I never thereafter met.

Under attending circumstances, our stay at home was made as pleasant as possible. Loving parents and sisters with fond hearts and willing hands united to make it such; but they could not hide their fears for our safety.

77

George's fate resulting from the act of a near-by enemy added fuel to their anxiety. My wound was healing very slowly—much more so than we had hoped it would, and all were loath to have us leave. We ended this battle royal between love and fear, when at the end of a week's stay, followed by benedictions pronounced by loving voices and coming direct from loving hearts, we left home for the last time, together, and started, by the way of Huttonsville, on our return to the army; necessarily traveling very slowly. My wounded side was far from well; I was still compelled to carry my broken arm in a sling, and we kept my rifle with us. Our sister Margaret had gone on to her home near where Valley Bend is now located, and upon reaching it we rested with her for a day or two, then moved on to Huttonsville. Here, as always, we were welcomed and entertained by our many schoolmates and friends residing there with a kindness peculiarly their own—a kindness now full of heart-felt sympathy on account of George's death. Good people! The vast extent of our gratitude for their kindness shown could have been measured only by that we felt for the sympathy given. With best wishes from all we, on the forenoon of October 9, 1862, again started on our way, reached, and stopped for the night at Mr. Aaron Bell's home on Becca's Creek.

Some time in the night our true old colored friend, Dick Green, came there and told us that the sheriff of our county, J. F. Phares, guarded by some 12 or 15 Federal soldiers had that evening passed up toward Mingo for the purpose of collecting taxes; that Captain Jacob S. Wamsley (I do not remember Wamsley's actual rank at that time) had organized a few men with the intention of following and attacking them, and wanted brother and me to join him. On account of my physical condition, as well as for other reasons, I felt like refusing, but Marion was inclined to go and we went. We found Captain Wamsley, with six or seven men, on Abraham Crouch's farm. None of these men, so far as I know, except our comrade Cy Crouch who was then on sick furlough, belonged to our army, and, with one or two exceptions, they were all virtually unknown to me. In the consultation then had, we learned that the enemy had passed on up the pike toward Mingo, and we agreed to go with the captain and his squad in pursuit. But we did so only because of a distinct understanding that we would not attack them at a friend's house or bushwhack them in the road without giving them a chance to surrender or fight, and, otherwise, to fight them wherever met. While the writer did not assume command of this expedition, yet this understanding was in accordance with his well known record throughout the war. It was dictated both by our wish to protect our friends upon whose innocent heads would fall the retaliatory wrath of our [enemies] for our alleged misdoings, of which fact we then had abundant proof; and because it did not seem right to us to shoot down a foe, no matter how bitter, without giving him a chance for his life. When it was suggested that our force would be insufficient, both in numbers and personnel to so fight the enemy, the captain informed us that others would join us before we overtook them.

We crossed the river and passed up through Mr. Hamilton Stalnaker's farm until near the pike just below the Elkwater fortifications where we stopped to load our empty guns. Marion walked on and, when we overtook him, was standing in the pike at the mouth of the hollow leading up to the home of our friend Mr. Alec Stalnaker, which stood some two hundred yards distant. We were not expecting the enemy there but Marion said he thought he had seen someone walking from the pike up to the house, where a light was now seen. We were unwilling to go on until we knew the enemy was before us, and went up the point of the ridge to the fortifications overlooking Stalnaker's house from the north. Almost immediately after getting there, we saw them silently leave the house and march in a body down toward the pike. Unquestionably they were then at our mercy, and but for the reasons above given, could and would not have escaped. We watched to see which way they would go upon reaching the pike. They apparently started back towards Huttonsville; and pursuant to our agreement, guided by some one who knew the ground and apparently forgetful of the smallness of our numbers, we hastily took a path by which we could head them before they could reach the Hamilton home.

We had gone some seventy-five or eighty yards, passing a cabin at some twenty or twenty-five yards, on our way, when some one called my attention to the fact that Marion was returning in the direction from which we had come. Looking back we could dimly see him walking rapidly back toward the cabin we had passed. At first we did not understand his reason for doing so; but looking more closely we discovered the enemy approaching the cabin from the farther side, and, followed by the others, I started after him as rapidly as I could go, but, hampered by the darkness and my broken arm, did not overtake him until just as he reached one corner of the cabin and the enemy had reached both its adjacent corners. We did not speak, but as I passed him on my way to meet the enemy on the right, the flash from his gun and that from those of the Federals on the left, apparently crossed each other in vicious challenge. If any shot came from the corner of the cabin to which I was approaching, I did not hear it and by the time I reached it the enemy were retreating. One of them was still quite near. I tried to use my gun but my wounded arm failed me. Cy Crouch, who had, doubtless, been by my side all the time, stepped forward, shot and the man fell heavily. Dropping the muzzle of my gun and drawing my revolver, we started to pursue the retreating foe. By this time all our men were up, and just then some one—I do not know who—laid his hand on my shoulder and told me that Marion had been wounded and the fight so ended.

We searched for Brother for some time, and to some distance, in the direction he had started—occasionally calling his name. In the mean time the enemy had left their severely wounded man at Mr. Stalnaker's and taking one less severely wounded with them had hastily retreated. When daylight brightened we went to the place where I had last seen Marion, and from there we literally trailed him by the precious blood he had shed to where we found him lying dead on the bank of a drain near Mr. Stalnaker's home, to which we carried him and laid him beside his mortally wounded enemy. The suddenness of his death disheartened me. A sense of utter loneliness enshrouded me. My future looked very desolate. My heart was almost breaking not only for myself alone but for the loved ones at home, as well. Again the morning zephyrs were whispering, "This is War," and it found an echo in our hearts. My own was filled with unspeakable sadness.

The citizen soldiers who had unflinchingly stood by us through the night had, at our suggestion, discreetly returned to their homes in the early morning. Cy, like the true comrade that he was, remained with me through all. Still with the object of protecting innocent resident citizens, I took upon myself the role of commander, which I had not in fact occupied in this transaction, and as such wrote to the Federal commander at Beverly over my own signature, telling him just what had occurred; that we as regular Confederate soldiers were alone responsible for it; that if he would send an ambulance and doctor without a guard, they could take their wounded man to Beverly, provided they would also convey Marion's body to our sister's home at Valley Bend, but otherwise that any force he might send would be attacked. On the next morning the doctor with his ambulance driver came alone and did as suggested. In the mean time, Cy and I had been joined by our comrade, G. W. Rowan, and alone we three watched them come and go. And so it was that Marion was laid to rest in the old Phares graveyard, where, and in the great Beyond, he was later joined by brother George and our dear parents. But what tongue can tell, or pen write, of the anguish with which this enforced parting filled the fond hearts of father, mother and sisters at the time it occurred? And who can truly measure the sorrow that filled my own as I went on my lonely way?

The circumstances attending Marion's death, as

above set forth, are absolutely correct; and I have thus minutely detailed them, because they were later partially misrepresented by someone, either purposely or because he did not know the facts. I can not explain, certainly, why he [Marion] turned back to the cabin as mentioned. I have no doubt that he saw the enemy coming toward it when he left us to meet them, and I have little doubt that he called our attention to it, but that in the hurry and noise we did not hear him.

CHAPTER XX

I RETURN TO THE ARMY—BATTLE OF FREDERICKSBURG

The past abided with and clung to me but my life and duty belonged to the future, and I started on my return to the army on October 15, reaching it in camp near Millwood, in the lower Shenandoah Valley, about 10 days later; having traveled slowly, somewhat painfully and part of the time alone. Here I found my company in good condition and excellent spirits. Although many had been wounded none had been killed in the Maryland campaign which had taken place in my absence, and in which they had taken an active part. This campaign had closed with the battle of Antietam, fought on September 17, and General Lee had then recrossed into Virginia and had spent the interval between that date and my return, in various camps between Winchester and the Potomac, resting, feeding, clothing, shoeing and recruiting his army with the result that it was now about up to its normal condition in strength and spirits, and ready to do any thing that "Uncle Robert" wanted done.

The first thing he wanted done before my return was the destruction of the railroad track in the vicinity of Harper's Ferry, and it was destroyed accordingly. About this time General McClellan had crossed into Virginia east of the Blue Ridge, and General Lee with General Longstreet's corps left the Valley and took position south of the Rappahannock facing his advance. General Jackson's corps, to which we belonged, remained for some time at Millwood and then proceeded, by easy marches, up the Valley and about the last of November crossed over the Ridge at Swift Run Gap, I think, and went into camp at its eastern foot for the night. We had passed by a still-house or two that afternoon and the boys of our regiment were rather boisterous—so much so that we christened our stopping place "Camp Row" and, almost from necessity, remained at it all the next day. Late in the afternoon Colonel Hoffman sent for me and I went to his headquarters, where we had a short talk. He said that it seemed to him that the drinking habit was growing among the men of the regiment and that he knew that I was opposed to drunkenness; and asked me if I could not suggest something that would assist him in putting a stop to it. I told him that the best way to do it would be to stop it first at headquarters and the men would follow the example set them. Here our conversation abruptly ended, but in the mean time I had observed the exact position occupied by the Colonel's jug in the rear part of his tent and later described it to comrade Tom Lewis. Next morning the Colonel had nothing stronger than coffee for breakfast, which Tom and his mess had. They said it was an excellent tapering off beverage.

We now marched to Fredericksburg where the rest of our army confronted that of General Burnside who had succeeded General McClellan.

On the morning of December 13, 1862, we took position on the right of General Longstreet's corps, thus making it the left, and General Jackson's the right, wing of our army. Jackson's front line was composed of artillery and General A. P. Hill's division; while our division, then commanded by General Early, was placed in rear of, and some distance from, that of Hill; our brigade then being commanded by Colonel Walker. Here we were held for some time after the battle commenced. There was some snow on the ground in the early morning and it was very cold. The first attack made by the enemy on Hill's front in the forenoon appeared to be easily repulsed, principally by our artillery; but about 1 o'clock in the afternoon, they made a more determined and sustained attack, and many of our wounded comrades were borne through our line, and we could tell by the sound of the firing that our men were rapidly retiring. Old soldiers will recognize this as one of the most nerve-trying positions in which men can be placed. At last we heard the welcome command, "Attention Brigade! Forward March!", given by Colonel Walker in a voice that must have reached every man in our brigade, and probably every one in our division. Apparently it came none too soon. We moved forward, met the enemy who had broken through Hill's line; drove them rapidly back to where they had broken it, on and across the railroad track, and to some distance in the fields beyond; killing, wounding and capturing many on our way; and stopping only upon a repeated peremptory order from our regimental superiors to do so. An order which we later learned General Jackson said should never have been given; because we were keeping so close to the retreating foe that he could not fire upon us with his cannon from Stafford Heights without endangering the lives of his own men.

Upon retiring pursuant to said order, the writer was not in the humor to kindly take the reprimand which Colonel Hoffman sought to give him for tardiness in obeying the same, and did not hesitate to criticize its giving. Our conversation on this occasion was not altogether pleasant. We had long since learned that the best and safest thing to do when we had our enemies, much more numerous than ourselves, on the run, was to keep them running with ever increasing speed until routed, and so I told the Colonel. I can truthfully say that I would much rather have faced the backs of two going Yankees than the face of one coming, or even standing. Yea verily! We were now formed in line along the railroad; but, for us, the battle of Fredericksburg had ended.

There was a slight hill on our right, upon which, as we took our position on our line, we could see General Lee and others less famous sitting on their horses; and observing among them some staff officers belonging to our own division, who were known to me, I joined them. It was a splendid position from which to view the battlefield. Away to the right, near Hamilton's Crossing, we could see the smoke arising, and hear the echoing boom from

Stuart's still rapidly firing cannon; while from our distant left, near Marye's Hill, we were greeted by a like sight and sound from those of Longstreet. Before us, and extending to the right and left as far as the positions named, we beheld in one vast panoramic view, nearly all that part of the battle-field upon which the enemy had maneuvered and fought. Their repulsed masses could be plainly seen, in irregular formation, on the plane near and along the river; while the fields in their front, and extending nearly to ours, were thickly dotted with their dead and wounded. It was an awe inspiring picture. The sun was hanging low in the west and a bitterly cold night was coming on. The was war at its worst.

While still on the slight hill mentioned, General Jackson, who did not appear as tranquil as usual, rode up and joined General Lee. The writer heard a part of their conversation, and from it gathered, or thought he gathered, that the former favored an advance upon the disorganized enemy at once, while the latter deemed that such a course would result in a useless sacrifice of the lives of his men, even if successful, which, (on account of the enemy's superior numbers and equipment

[Line(s) missing]

[su]preme effort but would attack again more determinedly, and if they did so his defeat would be more certain and disastrous, while their own loss would be much less, than could possibly be the case should he become the aggressor. He was always careful of the lives of his men.

While advancing pursuant to Colonel Walker's command, and before reaching the place where the enemy had broken through our front line, my schoolmate, messmate and long-time friend, the gallant Cyrus Crouch, fell mortally wounded. He died on the next day, and was buried and still sleeps near the battle-field.

Just as we reached the railroad, on our advance, a bewildered rabbit came hopping along on the track, and comrade John Folks, very coolly shot it. He was more hungry than angry, and preferred to kill it instead of a retreating Yankee. We were on short rations and ate it for breakfast next morning.

After the night had fallen, the northern sky was alight with the most beautiful aurora-borealis the writer has ever seen. Its glow continued far into the night. It was amusing to hear the various comments of the soldiers as to what it presaged. Superstition, seasoned with awe, was rife among them—so much so that we skeptics did not constitute a respectable minority.

The campaign in Virginia for the year 1862 virtually ended with the enemy's defeat at Fredericksburg, and we quartered in the Virginia woods near there for the remainder of the winter. About the last of March our regiment was ordered to report to General Imboden near Staunton and did so.

CHAPTER XXI

WITH GENERAL IMBODEN ON HIS WEST VIRGINIA RAID — 1863

We arrived at Huttonsville with General Imboden's command on the evening of April 23, 1863, and went into camp there. Soon after doing so, the General, who had just heard that Beverly was then occupied by a much larger force of the enemy than he was expecting, directed me to take a small detail of men, proceed in that direction, ascertain, if possible, the fact in reference to the number of said force, and report to him when and where met on his way next morning. The boys were tired from a hard day's march, but George and Squire Kittle and J. R. Apperson volunteered to go with me. We started at once, reached the homes of some friends near Beverly without trouble, ascertained from reliable sources the desired information, and, late in the night, started on our return. We had, so far, kept to the east side of the river but now crossed it, reached the pike near where Dailey is now located, and proceeded on our southward way just at dawn. We kept the pike until approaching the home of a rabid Union man, and fearing that he would, if he saw us, report our presence to the Beverly force and thus give notice of the coming of our army, we undertook to pass around his house unseen. We had gone but a short distance when we heard and saw a horseman, whom my comrades recognized as our sheriff, J. F. Phares—then almost unknown to me—coming toward Beverly at full speed. We tried to return to the road in time to stop him but failed, although he later admitted that he heard us order him to halt. All three of my comrades fired as he went rapidly by and one of their balls, at least, passed through and knocked off his hat, which we picked up; but

88

the writer ran on to the road and fired directly after him.

We knew at the time that he was wounded. but he pluckily kept his saddle until reaching the Federal pickets at the bridge about two miles distant, and there gave them their first information of our advance. We later learned that he had been fired upon at the Mill Creek bridge by our cavalry. Keeping the pike we now proceeded on our return, meeting and arresting on our way George Bradley and James McCall, both citizens, mounted, armed and hastening to Beverly to report our coming. We met our advancing cavalry near the present Valley Bend station, and leaving my comrades and our prisoners with them, I crossed the river to the back road, on Bradley's horse; found and reported to the General where he had halted his command which had just captured a Federal forage train with its escort. He seemed satisfied with our report that there were but 1,100 of the enemy at Beverly, and moved on; first giving me permission to ride ahead in search of the breakfast I had thus far missed.

When I overtook our skirmishers they were firing from the south, while those of the enemy were firing from the north, of the Washington Long residence, where I stopped; and while at first an occasional bullet struck the house, I was fearlessly and kindly entertained and sumptuously breakfasted by Mrs. Long and one of her daughters, who appeared to be the only persons about the dwelling.

By the time my appetite was appeased, and it took some time for that purpose, for I was very hungry, our skirmishers had moved on and I followed after; later joining my company on its advance near Beverly. Soon thereafter the enemy commenced to shell us from the hills south of the town and we were moved into the woods to our right, halted, and to our angry disgust, for some unexplained reason, left there until the retreat of the enemy from Beverly, which was burning as we passed through it in pursuit, had taken place.

Again with the permission of the General, I overtook and rode with our advance to Old Leadsville and then went home for the night. Here I found all well, and Mother's table and downy bed proved a complete requital for any inconvenience I had undergone in the last twenty-four hours. Returning to Beverly early next morning, I found the General still there with most of his command, and, in the conversation which followed learned that we differed materially as to what should be done with our citizen prisoners and their horses. I contended that the men should be released and the property returned to them, but the General was of opinion to, and did, send the prisoners to the Richmond prison and turned the horses over to the cavalry. My policy was not only right but best, as the sequel proved. The Federal authorities made reprisal upon our innocent sympathizers.* While in Beverly I called on the wounded sheriff, and found him doing quite well. In the mean time, however, we had captured his saddle pockets filled with properly signed but unpaid tax receipts, some of which we delivered to the parties against whom they were issued, and carelessly lost the rest.

Some time after the close of the war, Mr. Phares was sued, as sheriff, for not accounting for the money represented by these receipts, and summoned me as a witness to prove his inability, on account of the attendant danger, to collect it; and his counsel, Judge Woods, required me to give all the details of the transaction resulting in his being wounded. He was slightly offish with me for some time thereafter, but later used me as his principal witness in securing a pension as compensation for his wound. I was a competent and useful witness in both cases. Still later he and I became quite friendly.

When our army moved on west, a part of our company, under Lieutenant Perry Lewis, was left in Beverly to assist in caring for our captured and the army

---

* According to Maxwell's <u>History of Randolph County,</u> the Federals retaliated later in the summer by arresting 13 citizens and sending them to Fort Delaware. All but four died there. Sheriff Phares secured their release.

supplies already on hand; in gathering others; and in guarding and removing them and our few prisoners southward before the enemy should return.

The rest of our company moved on, through the rain, mud and hostile inhabitants, with General Imboden on his western march (which proved to be more wearisome than exciting or profitable), until we reached the vicinity of Summersville in Nicholas County. There permission was given to return by the way of Randolph and we started on our homeward way, rejoicing.

CHAPTER XXII

AGAIN IN MY HOME COUNTY AND AT HOME

Traveling hurriedly and principally by mountain trails, we reached Randolph County at Valley Head in a few days after leaving Imboden's command. Here we learned that Lieutenant Lewis with those of our company left with him in Beverly, all of whom had been purposely selected because they lived in, and north of, that vicinity, had already moved on South. All our squad, except the writer, lived in the southern end of our county—hence our reason for reaching it there. Promising the boys that when ready to start to Staunton, we would leave by Valley Mountain, and arranging to meet Lieutenant Wilson at Huttonsville, a few days later, we scattered, and, alone, I proceeded in that direction, pleasantly visiting among my friends on the way, and after arriving there. Lieutenant Wilson came as arranged. He was then on his way to call on the splendid Girl [Rachel Crouch] he later married, then living on the back road near Shaver's Run. While at Huttonsville we were joined by Ad[am] and Sam Wamsley, of Captain Marshall's Company.

Soon after starting we passed "Uncle John" Hutton's home and he told us that one Slayton, a noted Union scout, with some of his men, had come over Cheat Mountain and was somewhere in the neighborhood. None of us had ever seen Slayton, but "Uncle John", who was considerably excited, gave us a description of his general appearance, adding that he stuttered badly when talking; and we proceeded on our way. Just before reaching the end of the Lieutenant's journey, upon looking back, we discovered, in the distance, four men, with guns upon their shoulders, following in our wake. We were partly concealed by bushes and a bend in the road, and it was

92

evident that they had not yet seen us. So far as we knew none of our troops should have been on that road, and we naturally concluded that it was Slayton and his men, and, at once, concealed ourselves in the bushes on the upper side of the road. The oncoming men were marching in single file, and we formed in line so that each of us would. be opposite one of them when halted. Their leader accurately filled the description "Uncle John" had given us of Slayton, and we had no doubt of our ability to capture him, or, that he was the man we were after. When opposite to us, we called on them to halt. They stopped, and we ordered them to lay down their guns. They were quite slow in doing so, but when they saw that each of them was covered by one of our guns they dropped theirs.

Elated at making what, in view of Slayton's notoriety, we considered an important capture, we took charge of their guns and were discussing the disposition to be made of our prisoners, when their leader broke out in such a fluently flowing tirade, of great length, and composed principally of vitriolic cuss-words—all without pause or stammer—that we found it impossible to harmonize it with the halting speech of a stutterer, and upon investigation found that instead of Slayton and his squad, our prisoners were none other than Thompson Elza and others of Confederate fame. The drop in our feathers was observable; we parted with our one-time prisoners with mutual expressions of respect, and moved on. Leaving the Lieutenant with his girl, we arrived, without adventure at the home of the Wamsley boys, where we took supper. I was now sixteen miles from home; so far as we knew there was no intervening enemy, and I determined to take the main road through Beverly for that place.

Mr. Wamsley kindly lent me a splendid riding horse. I started on my way about 10 o'clock and reached home about midnight, without any trouble, although I ran into a depending telegraph wire, which for a moment gave both my horse and myself quite a scare.

All were well at home, where I remained for two

days; but having received some disquieting news about the return of the enemy to Beverly, I started on my return on the third morning in time to reach that place at dawn. Finding no soldiers there, I again called at the jail to see the wounded sheriff. I was armed and suppose my appearance was somewhat brigandish, for certainly Mrs. Phares was badly frightened at it, and it took the assurance of both her husband and myself to quiet her. The sheriff wanted me to stay for breakfast but I declined because of the still evident uneasiness of his wife.

It was well that I did so. By the time I was mounted, there was an unusual commotion on the main street of the town; and when I reached the southern end of it, the head of a Federal column was but a very short distance away—seventy-five yards at most—and I could now hear others coming by the street I had followed. They were all mounted, but I had perfect confidence in the speed of my horse so long as he remained unhurt. A few shots—harmless I think—were exchanged; a few commands to halt—useless I know—were given; and continued to be exchanged and given until we had gone, at no great rate of speed, to the Burnt Bridge two and a half miles above Beverly. Here instead of taking the back road direct to Mr. Wamsley's home, I crossed the river and took position among some willows on its southern side. The Yankees did not cross after me. Why I do not know, but, in addition to my revolvers, I had my Enfield rifle with me, and was vain enough, at the time, to think that possibly that fact had something to do with it. Anyway they followed me no farther, and upon seeing them returning to Beverly, I rode on to the home of my sister, near Valley Bend, where I took breakfast and dinner together, and later in the day crossed the river to Mr. Wamsley's, left his horse, took supper there, and walked on to Huttonsville that night. Here I found some of the boys awaiting me, and we started on our way South next morning. Going by the way of Mingo and collecting our comrades as we went, we joined our regiment in Staunton and our brigade near Fredericksburg, late in May; having met with no incident more unpleasant than that of riding through the soot and smoke on top of a train of freight cars through the Blue Ridge tunnel.

CHAPTER XXIII

REVIEW OF OUR CORPS—
MAKING READY FOR GETTYSBURG

On our return to the army from Western Virginia, we found that the natural elation which it had undoubtedly felt over its recent victory at Chancellorsville was overshadowed by its tremendous loss resulting from the death of its beloved general, Stonewall Jackson, to whom its achievement on that and many other battlefields was largely due. A loss which, although irreparable to, and sincerely mourned by, the entire army, was yet more deeply and personally felt by the soldiers of his own corps, for he had led them well and kindly.

About this time a reorganization of our army was effected. General Ewell was given command of General Jackson's old corps, which was composed of three divisions, numbered first, second, and third, commanded respectively, in the order named by Major Generals Early, Ed. Johnson and Rodes. We became the Third Brigade of Early's division under Brigadier General "Extra Billy" Smith.

Soon after the completion of this reorganization, a general review of our corps was held near Fredericksburg. Its three divisions, formed in double-rank parallel lines, and placed about eighty yards apart, were drawn up on an extensive plain. We were on the right of the first line and fronting us a short distance away a low platform, of considerable extent, upon which a small pavilion stood, had been erected. On and about it many spectators, mostly ladies, had gathered to witness the pageant. From this point General Lee, mounted on his famous horse, Traveler, accompanied by his cortege composed of some of his staff, Lieutenant-General Ewell, the three major generals above named and Lieutenant-General A. P. Hill, started, in a swift gallop, on his nine-mile run; greeted and followed, all the way, by martial music, ringing cheers and waving flags and handkerchiefs. His course led him along the front and rear of each of the division lines. One by one his escort dropped out of the race, and still the tireless gray, bearing his no less tireless rider, with undiminished speed, kept on and on until their starting place was won, considerably in advance of General Hill and one of General Lee's staff, who remained the only other contenders for that goal.

The enthusiastic greeting accorded rider and horse, was indescribable, and the writer will not attempt to describe it. Suffice it to say that it was a magnificent ovation tendered to the stamina of the horse, and to the incomparable grace and merit of the rider; enhanced and prolonged, as it doubtless was, by the fact that the General was received by many of the young ladies present on the platform, with smiles and kisses. The blushes of the General were quite observable; and the boys went wild at the sight. It was impossible to control them; and from one end of our line to the other cries of—"Hold on there!" "Stop that!" "Save one for me!" rang out in no uncertain tones, and continued until the faces of the girls, as well as that of the General, took on the hue of red roses, and those of the girls were as beautiful. Somewhat rude of the boys, perhaps, but very natural. They had the entire sympathy, if not the aid, of the writer.

This review was probably held to, in part, dispel the gloom caused by the death of General Jackson. If so it was successful, for the showing of the old corps both in numbers and eclat gave promise that its past record would be rivaled by that of its future.

A few days later we started on our Gettysburg trip; pausing in the vicinity of Culpepper Court House on the 9th of June, 1863, and listening to the near-by battle of Brandy Station, (Fleetwood), fought on that day between our cavalry and that of the enemy, resulting in a complete victory for our men. Again, with our corps leading, we took up our march, crossed the Blue Ridge at Chester Gap and our division reached the Valley turnpike at Newtown; where the writer, with a few of his intimate friends, were fortunate enough to be able to take an excellent dinner with kind old Aunt Mary and family, all of whom were delighted to again see our army in the Valley.

That same evening we fought our way, on the pike, almost to the suburbs of Winchester which was held by our old adversary, General Milroy, with about 9,000 men. Here we remained through the night, while the rest of our corps were being placed in position for the morrow's battle. On the next morning—June 14, 1863—leaving two of our brigades to engage the attention of the enemy in front, General Early, in person, by a detour to the left, along a secluded trail, led the brigades of General Hays and General Smith (ours), accompanied by several pieces of artillery, to an elevated plat of ground lying northwest of, and overlooking the outworks to the enemy's principal fort at Winchester; where, apparently undiscovered by them, we remained for some time, while other units of our army were being placed in the positions assigned them. It was here that the writer first had conversation with General "Extra Billy" Smith and heard him give his somewhat celebrated command of "Lay down 49th," being addressed to his former regiment, although now intended for his present brigade.

Hays' brigade, with ours as a support, were [sic] detailed to charge the works, and shortly before sundown, to the music of a furious duel between our artillery and that of the enemy, already beginning to grow slack on their part, we started rapidly on our way. Our cannoneers continued to shoot over, and very near, our heads until they could no longer do so, without endangering our lives. By this time our two brigades had commingled, and with the regular old Confederate yell, went over the enemy's works in one ragged line, capturing all their artillery and killing and capturing many of their men. The enemy were still resisting when we crossed over the embankment. One of Hays' men and I crossed it side by side. As we did so, he was met by a bayonet thrust which killed him almost instantly. While from a glance in front I comprehended his danger, I was not free to act in time to save him, and he only lived long enough to know that his death was avenged. I saw many men killed with the sabre, a few with musket-butts and clubs, during the war, but, strange as it now seems, only this one with a bayonet.

The artillery duel now commenced between the captured out-works and the main fort and continued late into the night. It was a grand sight; the course of the shells and balls could easily be seen by the light they emitted; while the sound they made apparently followed some distance in their rear. Lieutenant Lewis was then acting as adjutant for our regiment, and he told me, privately, that it had been detailed to lead a charge on the main fort early next morning. It was not a pleasant situation to anticipate, and, agreeing with Gray that, "Where ignorance is bliss, 'tis folly to be wise,"* we concluded not to enlighten the boys until it became absolutely necessary to do so. That time never came.

That night our regiment, with sentinels slightly advanced, bivouacked in said captured out-works, and some time before daylight, while most of the boys were sleeping—perchance pleasantly dreaming of far-away homes and friends, some of us, who, with a better knowledge of the situation, were more uneasy, discovered, to our great relief, that Milroy had taken time by the forelock and voluntarily evacuated the fort; and when we explained the premises to the boys, undoubtedly the retrospective view they then took of the disquieting situation of the preceding night was much more pleasant than would have been a prospective view at the time. Certainly it was decidedly so to us.

Be that as it may, Milroy had escaped in the night leaving in our hands some 4,000 sound prisoners; 300 loaded wagons; 600 head of horses; 27 cannon with their caissons; 5,000 small arms; a vast amount of military and commissary stores, and all of his severely wounded and

---

* Thomas Gray, "On a Distant Prospect of Eton College," stanza 10.

unburied dead.

Having thus rid the Valley of the enemy, we crossed the Potomac River at Shepherdstown, June 22nd, and our corps, marching slowly northward by the way of Boonsboro, Greenwood and Cashtown, reached York, Pennsylvania on the 29th, I think. We occasionally had slight skirmishing on the way, but nothing of special interest occurred. The citizens living along our route were for the most part, especially at first, inclined to be both afraid of, and hostile toward, us; but later learning of Lee's address to his soldiers directing and requesting them to do right, and that we were strictly observing directions, they became more friendly, and fed us, for pay, upon such excellent light bread, apple-butter and milk, that the boys nearly lost their hearts to some of the better looking Dutch girls who entertained them with such edibles. Some one has said that the shortest way to a man's heart is through his stomach; which would be especially true of men who had long been fed on half-fare in Dixie.

CHAPTER XXIV

BATTLE OF GETTYSBURG

As I remember it we bivouacked at or near York on the night of the 29th. It was here that the boys, aided by an auger and a hole in the bottom of a near-by freight car, extracted a supply of liquid refreshment from a barrel which they had, in some way, located in the car; but next morning when their hilarity excited the suspicion, or cupidity, of our regimental and brigade officers and our camp was searched for some of the refreshment, none was found; nevertheless, the potency thereof with the resultant exuberance of the boys lasted until late on the evening of the next day.

From York instead of proceeding towards Harrisburg as we expected, we took the road back toward Cashtown, and camped thereon that night. Next morning—July 1, we again started on our way there, but about noon inclined toward Gettysburg where we now heard fighting going on. Our brigade did not reach the battle-ground until late in the afternoon; consequently took but little part in that day's battle, which ended by the retreat of the enemy through Gettysburg about night-fall; and we went into camp near-by. Just before we did so, and while we were still standing in ranks, apparently awaiting orders to advance, several officers, including Generals Lee, Longstreet, Ewell and Early, I am sure, and others I think, held a consultation of some length, on a small knoll quite close to where we stood — so close that we caught the drift of their conversation, and understood therefrom that the enemy who had taken possession of Cemetery Hill would be attacked early next morning; and that General Longstreet would lead the attack.

It is not the purpose of the writer to undertake to describe the battle of Gettysburg, or to give the reasons for the repulse of the Confederate Army on that field. Many writers of history have attempted to do both, but have only succeeded in handing down contradictory statements resulting in failure. That General Lee there attacked a Federal force of superior numbers, having superior equipment and holding a superior position which he failed to carry, although he inflicted a heavier loss on the enemy than he sustained, is indisputable; but whether such superiority, or lack of concerted action on the part of some of his subordinate officers caused such failure, was not then, nor can it now be, certainly known, nor would it change the result if it were; but his reasons for the unexpected necessity of fighting this battle are satisfactorily given in his report thereof, are surely sound, and leave him blameless as a general.

Be that as it may, I shall only here speak of the limited part our brigade took in that battle. Early on the morning of the 2nd, we moved forward toward the enemy's entrenched position on Cemetery Hill until halted by a shower of grape-shot, from which we suffered but slight loss. We were then moved farther to the left, formed in line of battle facing said entrenchments, still in range of the Federal artillery from the effect of which we were somewhat protected by the formation of the ground, and ordered to lie down in position. Here we remained, inactive, for some time evidently awaiting, and expecting, Longstreet's attack on our right, which we heard planned on the previous evening, and ready to make our attack simultaneously with his. Afternoon came, but still no attack; and we were moved a short distance further to the left, about faced and, under fire both from the enemy's artillery and musketry, marched back toward where we had neared their entrenchments in the morning. On this return march our loss was considerable. The writer was, himself, slightly hurt by a bursting shell. We had halted at the time and a little later one of the boys was struck, well forward on the left side, by a musket ball. He had been standing at my side and as he fell I caught and held him up on bended knee and arm. We could see where the ball had entered through his jacket, and upon inquiry he told us that it had passed through his body, and that he could feel the blood running down his back from the place of its exit. Upon further examination, however, we discovered that the bullet had simply passed through his clothing in front of his body, upon which it left no mark. Notwithstanding he was a gallant soldier, our doctor, Bland, was inclined to think that the impact of the bullet with his clothing aided by a vivid imagination would have proved fatal but for our timely assurance that he was unwounded, and certainly his exhausted condition apparently sustained the doctor's opinion. This boy fought gallantly to the war's end.

We continued on our way, moving slowly and still in range of the enemy's guns, until late in the afternoon, when General Longstreet's cannon announced the commencement of his attack on their position to our right. We now moved forward more rapidly, but before overtaking the other brigades of our division, it, as well as Johnson's to our left, had, just as Longstreet's attack ceased, about twilight, become hotly engaged. For some reason, about that time, our brigade was detached from its division and sent to re-enforce that of General Johnson, which was now fighting on the slopes of Culps Hill, up which it was apparently driving the enemy. We found that some of his troops had captured and were holding their outworks, but we did not arrive until the fighting for the day was about over. Thus like D'Erlon's corps, which nearly a half-century before, alternated between Bonaparte at Ligny and Ney at Quatre Bras, we frittered away most of the day in useless marching.

At dawn next morning the enemy attacked Johnson in the position we had occupied for the night. As I remember it the Old Stonewall Brigade was in our immediate front, but in the repulse of the enemy which followed we lent some assistance and sustained some loss. We made a counter attack and drove them back until some of our men entered their main works at that point. Re-enforced they made several attacks, all of which we repulsed. In the mean while we were anxiously awaiting the sound of Longstreet's guns which were to be the prelude to his attack on our right. All there was quiet. About 10 o'clock, the overwhelming force of the enemy enabled them to flank us on the left with both infantry and artillery. We saw the movement but could not prevent it, and were compelled to fall back a short distance to a position which we held throughout the day. While some of the Stonewall brigade were on the line with us, we now faced the enemy at the distance of about three hundred and fifty yards, while our skirmishers, which were placed almost on our main line, successfully fought theirs who occupied a position near their line. We were so situated that we could see the effect of their shots. Their line of battle did not advance to attack us, but their artillery which had flanked us earlier in the day kept up a continual fire upon us, and while it did not prove very destructive, it did prove very inconvenient. As I remember it, three of their balls, in about as many minutes, one of which ruined his canteen, struck within five feet of the position occupied by Lieutenant W. H. Wilson, yet, while he naturally did some flopping, he gallantly held his post and fought back as best he could.

About 2 o'clock, preparatory to Pickett's coming charge, of which we were thoroughly cognizant, Longstreet opened his belated attack on the enemy to our right with all of his artillery. They replied in kind. Nearly 400 cannon engaged in this duel. Although at some distance from us, the air vibrated around us in waves and the earth quivered and trembled under our feet. It must have continued for at least two hours. Shortly after it began the pressure of the enemy upon us, both from front and flank, visibly decreased, and soon entirely ceased. This, to the writer, portended their withdrawal with the probable purpose of re-enforcing their line in front of Longstreet. Our brigade seemed to so understand the situation, and it was not long thereafter until the impatience of the boys because of their continued, enforced inactivity, found expression in requests to be led forward to attack the enemy in their front, in an effort to aid their distant comrades. In accordance with their wishes, the writer approached General Johnson, who was standing by his horse near-by (and whom we had all known since he commanded at Camp Alleghany), with the suggestion that it appeared to us that now was the time to attack the enemy in our front. He replied that he had no such orders. Probably my answer that "If Stonewall Jackson were here he would not wait for orders" savored both of presumption and impatience. Certainly the General looked as if he thought it did, but that was all.

Just after dark, when Pickett's charge was over, and quiet reigned away to our right, as well as in front of us, with the knowledge of our company, the writer stealthily advanced toward the position the enemy had held in our front, earlier in the day, and continued to do so until he arrived there, and found that it had been vacated. It was apparently a temporary breastwork built of logs. I, at once, reported the situation to General Johnson, but he said we were ordered to fall back to the position we had occupied on the night of the first day of the battle, and at 10 o'clock, slowly and undisturbed, we did so, and camped there for the night; taking position in line ready to meet the enemy should they advance, but they came not; nor did they show in any considerable numbers on their own lines until about 10 o'clock next morning.

Even then they manifested no disposition, whatever, to advance; and apparently inviting them to come, we faced them throughout the day ready to meet them if they came. During the night following, our army commenced to retire; General Hill's corps leading, General Longstreet's following and ours falling in the rear. We did not leave our battle-line until next morning, and still the enemy in our front had not advanced, nor were we disturbed by them, until well on our way to the Potomac. General Meade was foolishly censured for not making a counter attack to Pickett's or at least for not following us more rapidly. The fact was that the caution amounting to apparent timidity with which he advanced, was, unquestionably, dictated by sound military judgment, for he was not following a disorganized army but a regular fighting machine ready and willing to fight at any time and at any place determined upon by its great leader. Doubtless Meade's critics were all distant non-combatants.

We reached the swollen Potomac at Williamsport, on the 7th; succeeded in supplying ourselves with ammunition, of which we were greatly in need even when we left Gettysburg, faced the enemy north of the river until the 14th, and then crossed over into Virginia—our brigade locking arms and marching through water up to our arm-pits. A good bath which was not only refreshing but much needed.

Slowly, unbroken in spirit, and with undiminished faith in our great general, we made our way, unmolested, to our old position on and near the Rapidan River, where we arrived about the 1st of August, 1863, and again faced General Meade and his army.

CHAPTER XXV

AGAIN ON THE LINE OF THE RAPIDAN

Upon our return from Gettysburg, we went into camp south of and not far from the Rapidan River. Here we remained through the months of August and September facing, and almost continuously skirmishing with the enemy who held its opposite side, while we guarded the Raccoon and Somerville fords thereacross. The ground on our side of the river was higher than it was on theirs, and our skirmishers, who occupied slight entrenchments near the river bank could, for some distance, overlook and command the plain before them The enemy had no entrenchments near the river, but during the night-time they built barricades of rails at several points near the fords mentioned along the river bank, behind which they placed and undertook to keep their skirmishers by relieving them every night with relays from their distant line. They caused us some slight trouble and loss on the first morning after they had built these barricades before we discovered them, but we were now on the ground where, over a year before, we had learned that we could, by watching the smoke issue from their gun-muzzles, and actively making use of our entrenchments, dodge the coming bullets, and it was not long until the Yankees learned that mother earth made a much better shield than did fence rails; and after getting decidedly worsted, they left us for a few days in peace.

However, a little later, one morning we awoke to the fact that they had, during the previous night, strengthened and made their barricades bullet-proof and again had placed their skirmishers behind them. It was, therefore, our next move, and we moved. During the following night we brought up a few cannon, placed them where they could throw their bomb-shells and solid shot into their barricades, and doubled our skirmish line. When the skirmishing opened on the next morning, the fusillade with which we greeted the enemy doubtless surprised them, and certainly its effect was electrical. It was difficult to tell whether the fence rails from their barricades or the Yankees themselves flew the faster. Such of them as were able to do so left their annihilated coverts like coveys of partridges, and sought by flight to join their distant comrades. Many of them fell in their effort to do so; and many more would have fallen, had we not mercifully ceased firing and let them go their way.

This ended all further trouble between us and opposing skirmishers of the enemy so long as we remained in that position.

In the mean time the Federals had planted a battery near the edge of a tract of timberland, situated about a mile northwest of the river at Somerville or Raccoon ford, from which they had, while the above mentioned operations continued, kept up an intermittent fire upon us and upon our batteries behind us; and still continued to do so. Toward the last of September, while scouting around on the enemy's side of the river, we discovered that by taking advantage of the inequalities of the ground there, we could advance quite near to this battery without being seen by their pickets who were placed in the edge of the woods nearby; and reported that fact to Colonel Hoffman with the suggestion that with a small force we could capture this battery by attacking the men in charge of it at daylight on some future morning. When reported to General Early, he approved the plan and a few nights later I was placed in command of a squad of men, which we considered sufficient in numbers for the purpose, and directed to proceed as suggested. The greater part of our force was selected from our own company.

We waded the river just before daylight one frosty morning, early in October. There was no moon shining to light our way. We proceeded silently and cautiously until near the woods and secrecy was no longer possible, and then gallantly charged the foe. No shots greeted us. The enemy had fled—a fact about which we congratulated each other, as we advanced to take charge of those cannon which we intended to withdraw by hand until met by horses. But the only trophy won by our gallant and victorious charge was a Quaker-cannon, constructed of a smoke-stack, and arranged to grimly face us. Their artillery had been firing upon us from that position on the previous evening, and live coals, when we arrived, still glowed in the enemy's camp-fires; yet depression, instead of elation, stalked beside us as we slowly returned to camp. Nor did it easily depart from us, amid the chaff that greeted us. All that saved us even a shred of soldierly reputation was the fact that all of our comrades, like ourselves, had thought that the enemy still occupied the position charged upon. This eased us down some, but not sufficiently so to altogether quiet the boys, and it was some time before we heard the last of it.

CHAPTER XXVI

OUR COMPANY SUCCESSFULLY SKIRMISHES—THE WRITER IS THREATENED WITH ARREST AND HELPS BURN A PONTOON BRIDGE OVER THE RAPPAHANNOCK

About October 9, we left our quarters on the Rapidan River and started after General Meade, whose army was then encamped at Culpepper Court House. To the writer, this move then was, and still is, under the attending circumstances, a matter of surprise. Doubtless our men then, as always, were full of fight, but just as certainly their stomachs, haversacks and knapsacks were all very nearly empty. They had for some time been on short rations. Thousands of them were but scantily clothed in tattered garments, and almost an equal number were entirely shoeless or practically so. However, General Meade upon our advance hurriedly evacuated his position and retreated so rapidly that he reached his fortifications in rear of Manassas before we could intercept him, as General Lee had planned. Marching in the light order above indicated, probably we could have done so had not our meager rations entirely given out. We could not find green corn and apples upon which to subsist, as we had in this same vicinity, on our campaign against General Pope in 1862, and a halt of a day, while such rations as could be obtained were brought up, became absolutely necessary. This delay enabled General Meade to win the race.

Shortly after passing Warrenton our regiment, which was leading our corps, was halted and our company was directed to move forward and report to General Early. We did so, finding him, his escort and a cavalry skirmish line in front, facing the enemy's infantry skirmish line at a distance of about half-a-mile. The left of their line was protected by artillery and their right by what looked to us like, at least, a brigade of infantry, posted in the edge of a heavy growth of timber. We were ordered to clear that timber of the enemy and thus flank their artillery. The situation was by no means inviting. The ground between us and them was cleared and level; but we moved briskly forward, in column, until they opened, what appeared to us to be a very rapid and heavy fire, upon us. Then at double quick, in open order, we obliqued to the left; advanced our right, obliqued to the right, advanced our left, and when less than a hundred yards from the woods, went running, directly at it and the enemy—holding our fire until almost among them. The result was entirely satisfactory.

In this skirmish three of our men were slightly wounded and, as I remember it, two of the enemy were killed, a few wounded and several captured as we swept through the woods. The left of their line, with part of its protecting artillery, some of which was abandoned, had retreated when we closed on their right, thus leaving the road open, and in a few minutes after we emerged from the woods and gathered on the road at its farther side, General Early and those we had left with him galloped up. The compliments they paid us upon our action were evidently sincere; and one of the officers present—General Gordon I think—asked where we had learned the tactics used in advancing upon that woods.

On the day following this skirmish, in order to make it less painful to several of our company boys, who were limping along on bare and bleeding feet, I gave them permission to fall out of ranks, where the road was rough, and make their way as best they could on the grass or path by its side, and they did so. Colonel Hoffman noticed this breach of discipline, and in unscriptural language, roughly ordered them to take their places in the ranks at once. An altercation ensued, and by the time I reached the disputants the irate Colonel had learned that some of these boys could swear fully as well and even more fluently than he; especially the youthful Claude Louk, who appeared to be inclined to use his gun also. I hastened to inform the Colonel that the boys were so marching by my permission; that I alone was responsible for the situation, and was ready to abide the result; and then it was that he threatened, in positive terms, to have me arrested, and rode off apparently with that intention. A little later we saw him in consultation with General Early, while they occasionally looked our way. I was not arrested, nor were the boys, who were still picking their way, further interfered with. This was the fourth time the Colonel and I differed unpleasantly, principally on account of the way I cared for my men.

Returning from this expedition, our division, marching in the rear of the rest of our infantry army, recrossed the Rappahannock River near Rappahannock Station on a pontoon bridge, about the 4th of November, leaving General Hays' brigade in some old trenches on its northern side. I do not recall, perhaps did not, at the time, know, where the rest of our regiment and brigade were stationed, but our company was sent, as skirmishers, down on the south side of the river, to a position just below that held by the right of Hays' line on its opposite side. From there we witnessed the advance of the encircling lines of the enemy, which came on, almost in the form of a semi-circle, until both their right and left apparently rested on the river, thus completely enclosing Hays' brigade between it and their heavy lines. Why they did not advance upon his small force, and why it was not withdrawn, at once, was to us incomprehensible, but we thought that, as at Balaklava, some one was blundering, and while our skirmishers engaged theirs, posted on their left flank on the opposite side of the river, we still wondered. It was here that one of their skirmishers, with the benefit of a log to fire from and dodge behind, gave us considerable trouble, until Ed Kittle, who was also aided by a log and the smoke from my gun to conceal that from his, effectually stopped him. The distance between these logs was not less than three hundred yards.

In the twilight of that evening the enemy advanced in over-whelming force, charged and killed, wounded and captured some fifteen hundred of Hays' men, with a loss to themselves of some five hundred.

We were not relieved until about 10 o'clock that night. When we were, we marched up to the road running south from the pontoon bridge and halted. Seeing a small body of horsemen in our front, the writer joined them. Among them were General Early and Major Hale, with others whom I do not remember. They were discussing the danger of then attempting to burn the bridge. Some one had fired it earlier in the evening but the brands used had fallen apart and were dying out. Upon request I agreed to try to rekindle the fire, and gathering up additional fuel, advanced to and upon the bridge. I had been warned of danger, but all remained quiet and I proceeded to gather the half burnt material already there into a compact bunch, to fan it into flame and to feed it with the fuel I had brought, until I felt sure that my mission had been successfully accomplished. The bridge was now alight, and I felt like congratulating myself on my achievement and walking back to those whom I knew were watching me; but just then a volley of bullets coming, as it seemed to me, from at least a thousand rifles in the hands of the enemy stationed on the opposite side of the river, flew around and over me. The air about me seemed warm with flying lead, the wind caused by which apparently carried off my hat. It certainly had no hole in it when later examined, but it certainly, for some reason came off, for I picked it up and carried it out in my hand. Possibly it resulted from a duck which appeared to be the opinion of the boys. Be this all as it may, not just walking, perhaps, but unhurt, I rejoined my comrades, and our end of the bridge was burned by the rekindled fire. While nothing was promised me at the time for doing what I did, yet on the next morning, Major Hale, acting for General Early, offered me a furlough, which I did not then want or accept. He told me that the man who had first attempted to fire the bridge, who, as I remember it, was an artilleryman, had been promised some favor, the nature of which I do not remember.

We now retired, uninterrupted by the enemy, to our former position and short rations south of the Rapidan River, where we expected to build comfortable quarters in which to spend the approaching winter, of which we had already had a foretaste.

While on the above described expedition, we remained near Manassas Junction some three or four days before starting on our return. At the time, we understood that General Lee was considering the advisability of again crossing the Potomac, and that he was only deterred from doing so by the clotheless [sic] and shoeless condition of his men.

CHAPTER XXVII

BUILDING WINTER QUARTERS—
UNDER ARREST—MINE RUN CAMPAIGN—
WE GET A PRESENT—
WINTER OF 1863-64—TROUBLE IN CAMP—
I RESIGN AND LEAVE MY COMPANY

Upon returning to our old position south of the Rapidan River, we prepared to build quarters in which to spend the winter, which promised to be, and was, unusually severe. These quarters were to be constructed out of timber to be cut from the forest around us, and when finished would be quite comfortable. Colonel Hoffman camped with us and undertook to detail men, from the different companies of his regiment, to build his more pretentious cabin, a stable for his horse, and to chop and furnish wood for his fires. I refused, positively, to make such detail, and when he angrily persisted in his demand, told him in the plainest English at my command, that while my men had volunteered to fight, and were ready and willing to do anything required to enable them to wage successful war, yet they should not with my consent, as long as I could help it, unless willingly for compensation, be made private servants for him or anyone else. Then it was that the Colonel, with that mutilated short thumb of his thrust heavenward, as was his way when excited or angry, exclaimed, "Damn it sir! you can consider yourself under arrest." I first indirectly informed General Early of the situation and the reasons for it. No immediate action of which I know was taken but my men were not detailed for the purposes mentioned, while some others were. Later I addressed an explanatory letter to General Lee. Military rules required the Colonel to forward it, either approved or disapproved, through the regular

115

channels to the addressee. It was safe to assume that it went up with his disapproval; and so the matter rested for some days.

We thought that the campaign for the season had ended, and General Lee was, apparently, of that opinion; but about the 10th of November, General Meade advanced to Culpepper Court House, and a little later again faced us across the Rapidan. Our army, on account of furloughs granted, and small detachments sent off to forage, was now very much reduced in numbers, so much so that it is doubtful if we had present over 30,000 effective men. General Meade must have had more than double that number and doubtless knew our strength, at least approximately, as we knew his. General Longstreet, with most of his corps, was still in the South, where he had been sent to reinforce General Bragg before the battle of Chickamauga occurred.

As above stated, we had thought that the fighting for the season was over, but General Meade thought differently, and about the last of November broke camp and started on his Mine Run campaign. Our men were then only half fed, clothed and shod, but they were, as always, ready and anxious to again meet and measure strength with the enemy, who were now marching to flank us on the right. While preparing to do so Colonel Hoffman offered to release me from arrest. Of course I refused to be so acquitted of the charge against me; and told him that I would accept acquittal only upon the finding of a court-martial for which I had asked, or on an order from General Lee to whom I had appealed, but I further told him, that with his permission, and on account of the boys, not on his—a fact which I took occasion to make plain to him—I would, as a comrade, go with them. The permission was given and I went.

It was an unpleasant expedition, made more so by the inclement weather and by labor in constructing temporary breastworks while the enemy faced but hesitated to attack us. But little actual fighting occurred. For three or four days General Meade cautiously maneuvered in our front. Some slight skirmishing took place; but his timidity was so apparent that early on the morning of December 2nd, General Lee advanced only to find that General Meade, with a loss of nearly 2,000 men, was seeking safety by a rapid retreat, which could not be arrested south of the Rapidan, to which we followed him. Our loss was small; but several of our boys returned to their quarters with frozen feet.

Soon after our return, General Lee ordered my discharge from arrest, and at the same time, in a complimentary letter written and signed in his own handwriting, addressed to me, and handed down through Colonel Hoffman, completely justified my action. When this letter, which, by implication at least, necessarily contained an indirect reprimand for the Colonel, reached me, it was unendorsed by him.

While occupying these quarters on the edge of this great Virginia Wilderness; facing the grim future, which apparently held for us but little hope of temporal cheer or brightness; a religious revival, fostered by General Lee and others, commenced and continued for some time, and many men who had proved their gallantry on many battle-fields, now became and remained valiant soldiers of the cross. Several of our company boys joined the throng.

We were too far from home to expect gifts in the shape of clothing from loved ones there; but now, while others with friends less remote, were receiving such presents, it so happened that a box, containing two dozen pairs of hand knit socks, came to me from a patriotic society of ladies residing in and near Lexington, Virginia. It was accompanied by a letter written by their president—a Mrs. Miller I think—directing me to distribute the socks to the most meritorious men of my company. I failed to distribute them as suggested; and when I wrote thanking her for the present (which I did at once and in the best style of which I was capable), and telling her that my men were all so meritorious that I had found it impossible to distinguish between them, and had, therefore, given the socks to the most needy; she wrote me a beautiful letter commending my action, in reply.

Our mess now occupied a comfortable cabin, composed of one room, which served as bed-room, sitting-room, dining-room and kitchen; also a pantry which was quite small and usually empty. We had discovered while building that a wardrobe would be wholly unnecessary, therefore provided none. The writer slept in a nearby tent, on a bed of oak leaves, alone and comfortable throughout the winter. The rest of our company comrades fared about as did our individual mess. Even so situated the boys retained their good health and spirits; still, as ever, unflinchingly facing the lowering future with hearts "for any fate"*; yet, just then, Fate was grimly marching toward them, as all must have realized.

There was no way by which we could replenish our depleted wardrobes, but we cast about to devise ways and means by which we could supply food for our empty larders, and the manner in which we proceeded to do so was this. On the one hand, and near-by, there had been erected a temporary shed, under which certain commissary stores for the army, including many barrels of flour, had been stored. On the other hand stood the vast Wilderness wherein roamed deer, wild turkeys and wilder hogs which no one claimed. We now held a council of war, necessitated by the scarcity of bread and meat, at which it was determined that comrade Joe Snyder, whose qualifications for the purpose were excellent, with a selected squad, equally efficient, should, in the night-time visit the shed, and while he engaged the guard there posted in pleasant conversation, his squad should extract, from thereunder, a couple of barrels of flour; all of which was successfully accomplished, as was expected by us who knew Joe and his squad. At the same time it was determined that Ed Kittle, "Dixie John" Pritt and the writer, who still carried his Enfield rifle, should endeavor from the wild game mentioned, to supply the meat; which was to accompany the flour. On the first day out the writer

---

* H. W. Longfellow, "A Psalm of Life" stanza 9.

killed a three-hundred pound porker, and on the next two days we added two other hogs and a fine turkey-gobbler to our collection, but on the fourth day the woods were so full of amateur and noisy hunters, who had learned of our success, that the game all left our vicinity and migrated beyond our reach. However, it was astonishing how the rations thus gained eked out those doled out to us by our Government; for notwithstanding we now fared sumptuously every day, they tided us over and away beyond the holidays; which we pleasantly spent in growing the fat upon which, for the most part, we had to live during the coming spring-time.

Soon after the passing of the holidays, the harmony usually prevalent among us was, to some extent, interrupted by the untoward action of Colonel Hoffman. Our major, Cooper, resigned. According to the regular order of proceeding, Clawson, as senior captain of our regiment, was entitled to be promoted to fill the vacancy caused thereby. He was the choice of nearly all our commissioned company officers, was popular with our men, and thoroughly fitted to fill the position. However, Colonel Hoffman, disregarding alike Clawson's claims, merits and popularity, as well as our known wishes, for some reason and in some way, quietly and unexpectedly to us, succeeded in having his favorite, Captain McCutcheon of our regiment, promoted and advanced to fill the vacancy. Dissatisfaction and trouble resulted, and for a time discord, instead of harmony, reigned. Nearly all of our commissioned officers tendered their resignations from the service; and only withdrew them because of the friendly interposition and suggestions of our Honorable Secretary of War, Mr. Seddon, and of the patriotic magnanimity of Captain Clawson in backing him. Even so Captain Lyman of Company B, Highland County, insisted that his resignation be received and it was.

Later events proved to all of our regimental comrades that, beyond all question, we were right in our estimate of the soldierly merits of these two captains.[*]

We had hoped and thought that, by our concession in recalling our tendered resignations, all dissatisfaction engendered by the unpopular promotion of McCutcheon, with its consequent immediate result, would be finally allayed, else we would not have made it. But herein we were disappointed; for instead of recognizing as commendable the patriotism that induced us to withdraw our tendered resignations and, for the good of the service accept the unpleasant situation imposed upon us by his reprehensible pretentious course, Colonel Hoffman seemed to look upon the outcome of our trouble as a tribute to his exalted military attributes and actions, and to consider that it warranted him in continuing to mete out to us many petty annoyances, which, while possibly permissible, just hovered on the border-line of military etiquette—probably sometimes on its off side—until for myself and company, at least, it became almost unbearably oppressive. The Colonel had not forgiven me for refusing to allow him to impose upon or otherwise mistreat my men. Our trouble on that account first started while on General Stonewall Jackson's Valley Campaign; was twice repeated prior to October, 1863; was augmented in that month when I gave our shoeless boys leave to march on the grass by the road-side; and a little later reached its climax when I refused to detail them to work for him. Doubtless his animosity toward us (which apparently extended to the boys through me, as well as to myself), growing out of the last two incidents above named, was increased by the humiliating fact that both Generals Lee and Early sustained my action, thereby necessarily repudiating his.

Under the circumstances resignation was the only dignified, reputable course left open to me by military

---

[*] Here Harding may be referring to the fact that McCutcheon was elected to the Virginia General Assembly and excused from military duty in November, 1864 by Gen. Early. Originally, thirteen officers resigned.

ethics. For the two years I had commanded our company, no word had been spoken or act committed by any member of it, which had marred the pleasant association that existed between him and me; and no kinder, braver or truer men than those composing it ever fought and suffered together, for any reason or for any cause, and to separate now was almost unthinkable. Glorious boys! I yet take off my hat to the few of you who are still living, and to the memory of the many who have already crossed the "Great Divide" ahead of us. I remember you all as comrades tried and true, and think of each with a kindliness that is akin to affection. Ours was no ordinary friendship, but a friendship cemented by the ties which entwine around and bind together comrades who, side by side, have passed through perils which tried men's souls. A friendship cemented, not only by our own, but by the blood of many mutual friends who fell in battle beside us—perchance in our arms—which nobly and fearlessly doing their duty in fighting for the right as they then understood, and as we still understand it.

Yes, Glorious Boys! You were of the bravest and best, and always found worthy.

However, the unpleasant situation confronting us could only be relieved, if at all, by my resignation; and with the acquiescence of the boys because of such situation, I tendered it; at the same time writing a private letter to our war secretary, Mr. Seddon, giving my reasons for doing so. He approved my reasons but suggested a transfer with better rank. I declined and my resignation was accepted. Such transfer would have placed me among strangers.

When our enforced separation, which I still reckon among the saddest events of my army life, actually came, the boys prepared and gave me a written remembrance, beautifully expressing our mutual sentiments at parting, and the reasons which made it necessary. I thankfully accepted it; and my children still hold and prize it.

Yes, Glorious Boys! Here's my hand with my heart in it; as it was on that long-ago day when we parted on the border of the great Virginia Wilderness, in which so many of you later fell, found sepulcher in soldier graves, and now rest well.

Sorrowfully I went on my lonely way to seek, and make, other friends on other fields of action, but with a very pleasant recollection of, and keen regret at parting with, those I left behind.

Camps near Somerville Ford
February 5th 1864

General; —

I hereby respectfully tender my resignation "unconditional and immediate" as Captain of Company "F" 31st Regiment Virginia Infantry, my reason for so doing is the appointment, to the lowest field Office of our regiment; of a man whom I cannot respect nor trust as a superior officer, and feeling that it will be impossible for me to discharge the duties of a subordinate officer in an agreeable manner; I much prefer to serve in the ranks as a private soldier.

Most Respectfully your
Obt. Servt.
Joseph F. Harding Capt.
Co "F" 31st Regt. Va Infty.

General S. Cooper
A. & I. Genl.

Harding's Resignation Letter, February 5th, 1864
Approved by Headquarters ANV
For Gen. R. E. Lee by W. H. Taylor
February 11, 1864
Original in The National Archives

CHAPTER XXVIII

IN THE CAVALRY—
A SKIRMISH IN MY HOME COUNTY

Leaving my old company early in March, 1864, I arrived on Knapp's Creek, Pocahontas County, [West] Virginia, about the middle of that month. Here I found Captain Elihu Hutton's Company C, Twentieth Virginia Cavalry Regiment. Several of my former schoolmates belonged to this company; among them Eugenius Hutton, who had belonged to my old company, which he had left to accept a lieutenancy in that of his [brother's]. He had been one of my chums while with me, and I now joined his brother's company. Colonel Arnett now commanded our regiment, and General W. L. Jackson our brigade; and notwithstanding it was supposed to be guarding the roads approaching from the west, yet, for the purpose of obtaining food and forage, it was separated into small detachments, which occupied camps at considerable distances from each other. Ours was called Camp Northwest. It was not commodious, nor was our grub of the best nor plentiful. Winter weather continued until late in April. Discipline was slack and about the middle of that month Lieutenant Gene and I obtained permission to scout toward home. Indeed our commander was anxious for us to go; especially in that direction.

We arrived at Elkwater without adventure; spent a day visiting in that community and then proceeded to Gene's home at Huttonsville; where he was accorded an affectionate, and the writer a kindly, welcome by his mother and sisters, and where we fared sumptuously during our stay. It was all very enjoyable after our hard life and short rations at Camp Northwest, and we stayed there a few days, one of which was Sunday. On that day a local exhorter held religious services in the large, home sitting-room, and our concealment was necessary. At one side of this room an open stairway ascended to an alcove above, from which we could hear, and by the exercise of caution, partly see without being seen what took place below; and here Gene and I ensconced ourselves before the congregation assembled. Just before the exhorter opened the services some twelve or fifteen Yankees rode up, hitched their horses to the yard fence, came into the room, found seats, and piously remained until the exhortation was ended and the congregation dismissed. Their deportment throughout was of the best, and when, upon being dismissed, they quietly rode away, we knew them to be gentlemen, notwithstanding they were, at present, our enemies.

Most of those who resided near-by, also left when the services closed; but a few remained to dinner; among them Mrs. McCall, whose husband, mounted on his fine horse, had been captured on Imboden's raid, and both man and horse sent South. This event, in which Mrs. McCall knew that we—especially the writer—had taken part, had increased her former bitterness against all rebels in general and against us in particular, as we had recently learned; and we now arranged with Gene's sisters and some of their girl friends then present, to encourage her to talk about us and they did so. Gene and I from our hiding place could hear all that was said. The old adage that an eavesdropper never hears any good said of himself, was here unquestionably verified. From first to last that old lady abused us in the most unorthodox, vitriolic language invented for the use of ladies. Her vituperation, however, all seemed to be on account of the loss of the horse, and no mention was made as to that of the man. We enjoyed the situation immensely.

Soon thereafter we started on our way to my home, where by familiar paths, we arrived, without trouble, on the following day. Here we were welcomed and entertained much as we had been at Gene's home. About the only difference being a reversal of our positions in the affection and kindliness of our respective families. Doubtless our enjoyment of the good things to eat set before us, and other comforts received at our homes, was enhanced by a recollection of those we had missed at Camp Northwest and elsewhere. For if a "Sorrow's crown of sorrow is remembering happier things" be true, why is not its converse also true?* We certainly remembered getting worse things.

After remaining quietly at home a few days, we returned to Huttonsville and thence by way of Mingo to our command, which we now found camped at Hightown and Crab Bottom in Highland County, where it had been moved in our absence. Our own company was camped near the Pendleton County line, where, on account of a report that the enemy were about to advance from Beverly by the North Fork road, they were picketing that route.

When Gene and I reached camp at Crab Bottom, we found our officers somewhat uneasy over the report of the enemy's advance from Beverly. We assured our colonel that while General Harris, who commanded at that place, was, and doubtless would be, occasionally sending out small scouting—probably marauding—parties, yet we were confident that he had no intention of advancing upon us with his small force, and if he did we could whip him. Our report did not appear to satisfy him, and about the 6th of May, the writer was directed to take a small detail, composed of such number as he deemed best, and return to Beverly to ascertain the truth in the premises. The fact that Federal foot-scouts, especially Slayton's squad, usually hovered on the way, made it necessary that we should also travel on foot. If we hurried, as would be best, none of my cavalry comrades could keep pace with me, so I concluded to go alone; but just when starting early in the morning, Fred White, who had in some way obtained permission to go along, joined me. It was too late to prevent his going, without losing considerable time; and together we proceeded, going by the way of Hightown and Camp Alleghany. Our advanced cavalry picket was posted

---

* Quote is from Tennyson's "Locksley Hall," line 76.

a short distance east of this Camp and until we passed it we were in but little danger from the enemy. From here on caution was necessary, and leaving the pike we traveled south of it by unfrequented trails; crossed the Greenbrier River a short distance above where Cass is now located; and proceeded thence by the eastern face of Back Alleghany Mountain to the pike at Slaven's Cabin. From here on across Cheat Mountain, traveling quietly and warily until we reached its western top, we kept [to] the pike. Fred was now getting very tired, and occasionally lagged behind; which, under the circumstances was not objectionable; but when we again left the pike and took the paths down the western face of the mountain, at my suggestion he stopped at the first available house and I did not again see him while on that trip. I arrived at the home of Alf. Hutton late in the afternoon, having walked fifty-three miles in about eleven hours. Later when I was inclined to boast of having walked fifty-three miles in less than a day, mostly by mountain trails, going in the direction of the Yankees, carrying my Enfield, and always on the lookout ahead, the boys, with some truth in the suggestion, would head me off by adding, "And the Lord only knows how far you could have gone in that time if you had been traveling in the other direction."

We had theretofore established Alf's home as an underground news station, and now upon my arrival there, I learned that several of Captain Marshall's men, under Lieutenant J. S. Wamsley, had, after Gene and I went out, come in by the way of Mingo, and were now visiting their homes near and south of Huttonsville. I did not see any of them, but they were informed of where I then was and of my contemplated movements for the next twenty-four hours. After a sleepless night, alone, I started, early next morning, for Beverly; traveled in a round-about-way, on bypaths and through the woods, and arrived in that vicinity about noon. Was, at one time, on a hill, from whence I could overlook the town and Federal camps. Having obtained all the information obtainable, or necessary for the accomplishment of my purpose, I retraced my way to Huttonsville. The dry leaves under foot in the ridges made it hard walking and it was after night-fall when I reached there; and learned that late in the afternoon a Federal cavalry scout of about 50 men had arrived there, fed their horses, eaten supper, and gone on over the mountain to Greenbrier River; and that Lieutenant Wamsley was collecting his men with the intention of following them. We knew of this expedition while near Beverly, but did not expect it to go beyond Huttonsville. Wamsley sent some of his men after me with a request that I join him. I was very sleepy—possibly a little tired—but I went; found him with his men on the pike, and consented to go along under him, as a private volunteer. None of my company were with us. We followed the pike until we reached the first top of Cheat Mountain. Here we built a barricade across the pike. The Lieutenant placed a picket some distance in advance, with orders to conceal themselves by the roadside, shoot at the enemy as they were passing, and run them into our blockade where we could and would capture them; and we then lay down to rest and watch.

The plan promised well, but the Lieutenant had failed to reckon with old Morpheus, into whose outstretched arms, as soon as quiet reigned, we fell, in sound and dreamless sleep. For the writer this was the third successive night, practically without sleep; and Wamsley's detail—in all twenty men—were about in like situation. I awoke to the sound of the foot-fall of horses mingled with that of a near-by voice exclaiming, "Here's something that wasn't here as we came over." Mentally I was wide awake at once. Physically my body and limbs were, for the moment, sound asleep, and I was wholly unable to rise or even to use my arms; but my hand which rested on the lock of my gun began to tingle at the finger tips, and the sensation of pricking and thrilling caused by blood-circulation [began] to permeate my arms. Although it was early gray-dawn, the enemy did not yet appear to comprehend the situation, and one of them jumped his horse up on the road bank and undertook to cross over the butt of the log, out of which our barricade had been constructed, just where I had been lying behind it. He was too late. Although not yet able to rise to my feet I threw my gun forward past his horse's head, with its muzzle within six inches of his own breast. It was cocked and my finger rested against the trigger. We were looking directly into each other's eyes. No doubt we presented a first class tragi-comical picture; but, as quietly as possible I said, "Don't run, sir, or I will kill you." He blanched a little, but exclaiming, "Oh please don't kill me," turned his horse as he spoke, and on a dead run joined his already retreating comrades. I did not try to shoot him as he went. He had unwittingly given me too great an advantage over him to be fairly used, and I let him go. All this must have occupied but a very few moments, because none of my comrades, who had been sleeping in various near-by positions, awoke to action in time to even wound a man or horse, and our picket only slightly wounded one horse as the enemy ran by. The whole incident had resulted in an egregious fizzle, for which no one was more blamable than was his fellow. We had, however, captured one excellent, slightly wounded horse, had ourselves lost nothing but a little self esteem, and were, therefore, still slightly ahead. With a view to keeping this lead, Lieutenant Wamsley, with Jacob O. Ward and the writer as his advance guard, moved forward in pursuit of the retreating foe.

Jake advanced through the timber above and at some distance from the pike so as to be able to uncover the position of any lurking enemy watching it. The writer walked on the pike, near the high bank at its upper side, the inequalities of which afforded him considerable concealment; and the lower side of the pike was protected by thick laurel. Keeping some two hundred or three hundred yards in advance of our command, we reached a point some distance west of the Red Run Bridge. Attracted by a slight noise apparently coming from the bridge, the writer stopped. About one hundred and twenty-five yards ahead the pike made a considerable bend, and before I could communicate with Jake, a Federal soldier, also seeking the protection of its upper bank, came cautiously in sight and stopped at the bend. He saw Jake instead of me and partially raised his gun to shoot. Mine was already at my shoulder, but he lowered his, still apparently watching for Jake, and I did not then shoot. Momentarily scanning the woods for my comrade, I discovered that he was advancing by an old road that dropped off into the pike just where our enemy, whose body was hid from him by the bank, was standing. The Yankee turned and spoke to some one behind who was not in sight. Under the circumstances "watchful waiting" was not good policy, perhaps, but for the moment, and only for a moment, I followed it.

As Jake again stepped in plain view of him, the Yankee again raised his gun for a shot that could scarcely have missed. My gun spoke and he did not shoot. We never knew just what was the result of my shot. We heard the man, as he apparently fell into the arms of his comrades behind, loudly exclaim that he was killed, and to continue his complaint as they rapidly bore him away, and almost immediately we heard their horses crossing the bridge in hasty retreat; but while we found some evidence of the skirmish, near to and in the rear of where the man stood, we found no one there, either wounded or dead. I do know, however, that just as I shot, I caught sight of the brass buckle on the U. S. belt that encircled the man's body, and am of the opinion, and hope, that the ball sped true, struck that buckle, and glanced off. Such a jar, would, for a time at least, lead any one to think he was killed; but I now hope this one was mistaken.

We saw nothing more of the enemy, although we followed them as rapidly as we could until they left the pike on the eastern face of Back Alleghany Mountain. Thence by a trail along the face and the Harper trail they reached Beverly. As to whether or not they all returned, the information we received was contradictory, and we can only hope that they did.

In its main features this incident held for me a pleasant sequel. So far as I remember, the Yankee who asked me not to kill him and I never again met, but each of us later learned who the other was. His name was Mat Quick, a resident of our county. When I was a candidate for sheriff in 1876, both he and Jake Ward supported me, and both gave as, at least, one reason for doing so my action during this Cheat Mountain skirmish. Both were gallant men.

Next day I reached camp at Crab Bottom, alone, made a satisfactory report of my trip and that night slept well.

CHAPTER XXIX

MY FIRST COMMAND OF A DETACHMENT OF CAVALRY A CRITICAL RECONNOISSANCE—WE MEET A NOBLE-HEARTED WOMAN

After considerable maneuvering on different fronts, our brigade was assembled near Callihan's Stand, Bath County*, about the last of May, 1864. It was then guarding the roads leading from the vicinity of Lewisburg on which the Federals, under Generals Crook and Averell, were advancing upon Staunton to meet General Hunter. This was the first time I had seen all the units of our brigade together. It was very small, and certainly did not comprise more than 1,000 badly mounted and equipped men—not enough to make a medium sized regiment. In the meantime, I had been elected lieutenant by our Company, and about the first of June was placed in command of a detachment of 12 or 15 men, mounted on Captain Hutton's horse, Stonewall, and directed to advance on the road by which the enemy were approaching until we met them. Our orders were to start at a certain hour and travel at a certain rate of speed, with the understanding that we were to be followed and supported by the brigade, which would govern its movements by ours, as ordered.

In the early morning, with two men some three hundred yards in advance and two others at about half that distance, we moved forward, as directed, and so continued for some seven or eight miles. We had passed over a wooded hill and then straight across a plain between one and two miles when, just at a bend in the road, our advance guard met the enemy and shooting

---

* Callihan's is in Alleghany County, VA.

commenced. It was an awkward situation. Our guard fell back at once, followed closely by several hundred splendidly mounted cavalry, who from the formation of the ground could, as they came round the bend, plainly see the smallness of our unsupported force. There was nothing to do, but to shoot and run, and we shot and ran, especially ran, accordingly and fast. It would be hard to tell which was the worse scared, Stonewall or the writer. He stood up on his hind feet while I told the boys to get back to that wooded hill in the shortest possible time, and we all got. However, Stonewall and I managed, by dint of a good deal of physical and mental effort, to keep between the Yankees and the rear of our own men. It was fortunate for us that many of the leading files of the enemy emptied their guns at us in the beginning of the race. By so doing they not only rendered themselves less dangerous, but now, as they closed upon us, shielded us from the guns of their more distant comrades.

The writer started on that run with two revolvers carrying twelve bullets. It was not best to carelessly waste them, but occasionally, in an effort to check the enemy, he doubtless did so. We—Stonewall and I—kept our position between our men and theirs until we had neared the foot of the wooded hill mentioned. We had several times turned, faced and attempted to halt them. At first it had some effect; but now, apparently concluding that our guns were not always loaded they had closed up until very little turning room was left; and, for the first time giving Stonewall the rein and calling to some of the boys who were farthest behind to abandon their winded horses and take to the woods, I reached the top of the hill in time to halt some of our leading men, who gave the enemy a volley. I then told them to continue on the run. Stonewall and I still faced the oncoming foe. He again stood up on his hind feet while I finished emptying my pistols. I could have done better if Stonewall had. The enemy came within a short distance of us, did but little or no shooting but used some secular language and then dismounted and advanced toward us on foot. Although they still marched forward, the race had ended and Stonewall and I left them there. In his biographical sketch of Colonel Hutton, given in his Randolph County History, Maxwell says that I lost ten men in this skirmish, but the truth is that I did not lose a single man. Some three or four horses were captured, but all their riders had escaped to the woods, as directed. Our horses were broken down while those of the enemy were in good condition. We did well to escape as we did.

Some three or four miles from Callihan's I met Lieutenant Gene Hutton, who informed me that, for some reason, our brigade had not followed us in the morning, as planned, that it was now moving toward Covington, that some of our detail had already reached camp with the news of our meeting with, and the advance of, the enemy, and that the general requested that we ascertain as near as possible their exact number. Sending our horses back by his comrade, he and I concealed ourselves in some shrubbery on a hillside near the road. In a short time the enemy commenced marching by. Their rear passed us just at dusk. We counted them accurately—their infantry and cavalry almost by file, and their artillery by the piece—setting down the number on paper at the time. I do not remember the numbers, respectively, of these component parts, but the army aggregated about 12,000 men.

After night-fall we started over the hill in the direction of Covington, but had gone but a short distance when we discovered, by the fires at which they were cooking, that the enemy had established a cordon of pickets between us and that place. We lay down and slept until nearly daylight, and then advancing rapidly, and firing upon one and passing between it and another of the picket posts, we joined our command and reported. Our brigade now moved by a road nearly parallel to that upon which the enemy were advancing, headed and skirmished with them, but, of course, could not stop them, and they joined General Hunter at Staunton, while we marched south of that place and joined our small army.

About the 10th of June, 1864, we were stationed on a road—probably the main road—leading south from Staunton some little distance from that place. On the evening before General Hunter left there for his raid on Lexington and Lynchburg, our brigade, or part of it, accompanied by General W. L. Jackson, made a reconnoissance toward Staunton. About two miles from there, in the early part of the night, we ran into, charged upon and captured a Federal picket, which was apparently just getting ready to leave its post. Here the main body of our command was halted, dismounted and left, but a detachment of some twenty men, mostly from our county, still accompanied by the General moved forward on the road, until within about a mile of Staunton, parts of which were evidently on fire. The situation was ominous and we halted. Several refugees from Staunton were with us and the General now asked that some of them go into the place and learn what was going on, while the rest awaited their return. They all declined, and he then asked me to go. I was wholly unacquainted with the town, but agreed to go if furnished a guide. After some hesitancy, one of these refugees, whose name I have forgotten, except that they called him John, consented to guide me, saying at the time that if he could reach the home of a certain lady friend, he was sure he could obtain the necessary information from her.

Keeping near the road we at once moved forward; soon entered the outskirts of the town; passed over some vacant lots, by burning houses and the debris of lately abandoned bivouacs; and thus came nearly to the railroad, along the line of which many buildings had been burned so recently that they still smoldered. John now pointed out the house wherein resided his lady friend. It stood at the junction of the road, or street, by which we came with one that ran westward therefrom, upon which, aided by the light of the fires ahead, we could now see a long line of soldiers in blue marching westward, while others from the north and east, still entered it. John here began to show signs of timidity or treachery—for the moment I could not tell which—and insisted that we could not get to the house, standing as it did within less than ten steps of where the enemy were so marching. However he was induced to try. It was rather a large house, with a long porch to the main building, facing the east, and a double-porched ell facing the south. As we came around the end of the house to this long porch, a large dog barked and bounded along it toward us, and some one entered the house. John now seemed inclined to run, but an encircling arm and a pistol encouraged him to move onto that double-porched ell—the goal he had told me he was striving for—and when we reached it a woman was standing on the upper porch. She recognized John by his voice. It was now nearly daylight, and we lost no time in telling her what we wanted to learn. In a sweet low voice, that trembled just a little at first but soon steadied, in brief sentences she told us that some of the Federal generals were sleeping in the main building below; that they took supper at her table on the previous evening and discussed their plans while doing so; that they were going to Lynchburg by the way of Lexington and had now started on their way; that the road upon which we could then see and hear them marching would intercept the one by which we came a few miles south of Staunton, and that she understood they numbered some 20,000 men. Glorious woman! Apparently her only anxiety was because of our danger. She did not falter or hesitate, as she gave us this information. She did not seem to count the danger to herself. Both her tone and manner bespoke the highest order of culture, bravery and patriotism. We could not see her face but I know it must have been beautiful. The information that she gave us proved to be absolutely true. Indeed coming from the source it did—from a patriotic woman's intelligent mind and true heart—it could not have been otherwise.

Unmolested, we returned rapidly to our command, found the General with his advanced detachment where we had left them and reported. We immediately fell back toward Lexington, barely reaching the road, which the lady said would intercept ours, in time to skirmish with and pass the head of the enemy's advancing column.

While returning, of course I apologized to John for my rudeness while in Staunton. He was, however, generous enough to say that my conduct, in view of his action, was entirely excusable. Upon the whole he seemed to look upon the transaction, and his part in it, with some pride. While possibly a little timid, because of the novelty of the situation, yet he was true to his comrade.

At parting he gave me, in writing, his name and that of his lady friend, but I lost them at some time during Early's Valley campaign, and, depending upon that writing instead of memory, have forgotten them.

But while I have forgotten her name, yet faithful memory retains, and always will retain, a vivid impression of the individuality of that noble woman, as, impelled by a love of country and constitutional liberty, she stood almost in the presence of her country's enemies, and gave us this information for the purpose of undoing them.

A remembrance of her, and such as her, is, and will remain, among the proudest heritages of her own loved South-land.

CHAPTER XXX

AFTER GENERAL HUNTER IN JUNE, 1864— CAVALRY CHARGE AT SALEM, VIRGINIA— WITH GENERAL EARLY TO WASHINGTON— A SKIRMISH AT ROCKVILLE, MARYLAND

Our little army of cavalry then commanded by General Echols, I think, although almost frenzied by General Hunter's acts of vandalism, could do but little to stay or retard his march to Lexington and Lynchburg. We did what we could; continuously hovering in front of, and frequently striking at, the heads of his advancing columns, whose paths were heralded by the lights reflected from burning public property, and private homes, granaries, food and forage supplies; thus making them easy to locate, and leaving ruin, desolation and an insulted people, behind them. And so we came to Lynchburg, met General Early, with his little army, there, and turned back. Now the Hunter became the hunted—apparently the haunted. He did not, like the man from Thermopylae, fight and run away, because he ran without fighting at all. The inquisitive reader of history, in searching for the reason why he ran, must, in the absence of any other, conclude that it was because he was no exception to the rule that, "Conscience doth make cowards of us all."*

Hunter's conscience, if any he had, when remembering the ruined homes, devastated farms and cruel desolation he had made and left behind on his forward march, and must repass upon his return, must have borne heavily upon him, and the fact that an avenging nemesis, in the shape of General Early with his little army, was before him, added to his trepidation, and so he ran. His army was about double that of General

---

* Shakespeare, *Hamlet*, (III, i, 83)

Early's in both numbers and equipment, and about equal in everything else, except in the character of his officers, the character and ability of their leader, and the quality of right-doing in both. Still he ran. Ran at once and so fast that, with the exception of some very light skirmishing, we did not overtake his rear-guard until we reached the town of Salem.

Here the writer, who was now well mounted, took a humble part in his first cavalry charge. The enemy had planted several pieces of artillery in and near the town, supported by detachments of both infantry and cavalry holding good positions. None of our infantry were yet up and we did not wait for them. I do not remember who had immediate command of us. Major Harry Gilmore [sic], of Maryland, was riding just to my left. Some one—possibly several at once—yelled "Charge" and away we went, on the run from the start. The enemy had been pushed back until we were less than four hundred yards from their cannon when we started to charge. After giving us one volley, their cavalry and infantry had retreated. We made no halt, and their artillerymen did not have time to retreat before we were among them. Their last volley was of grape-shot. It was delivered when some of us were less than thirty yards from the muzzles of their guns. The air seemed rife with their leaden hail. The wind caused by their discharge blew in our faces, and the earth quivered and trembled under us. The vibrations around us apparently staggered, but did not stop, our horses, and pandemonium, for the moment, seemed to reign. Still it was all more scary than hurtful, for our loss was small. We thought then, and I still think, that those artillerymen expected that volley of grape-shot to check us, and so stood their ground longer than they, otherwise, would have done. They were mistaken. We were among, and had captured, them, as well as their cannon, almost before the echoes therefrom had ceased to reverberate from the adjacent hills. Major Gilmore, whom I had met at my aunt's at Newtown, now rode up, shook hands, and, in company with others, we started on after the retreating foe, picking up several of his infantry on our way.

Our advance detachment halted and went into camp at night-fall; but, by direction of our colonel, Buck Carter of Barbour County and I left our horses and, on foot followed the retreating enemy through the entire night. Our orders were to follow until we came up with them. This we did not do until just at early dawn next morning, when we came upon their rear-guard, which after the exchange of a few shots, hurriedly retreated. We took breakfast—also a nap—at a near-by house. It was after noon when our command overtook us. We then followed the enemy, on their way to the Ohio River, for a short distance farther, overtook and had another skirmish with them, in which they were again worsted, and continued on their run. We then left their trail, and joined the rest of our army at Harrisonburg in the Shenandoah Valley. Here I found my old company and regiment in General Ramseur's division of General Early' s command. The boys gave me a hearty welcome, and we spent a few hours then, and frequently thereafter during that campaign, very pleasantly together.

After our brigade left the retreating enemy in the mountains of Western Virginia, it did not pass through Lexington and Staunton on its way to join the rest of our army at Harrisonburg; consequently we did not see the worst of the Hunterizing which laid waste, and made desolate, the beautiful and fertile Shenandoah Valley; but as we moved on toward the Potomac River, evidences of it could be seen on every hand, and the victimized residents, with tearful eyes and grateful hearts, welcomed us to their ruined homes, as temporary deliverers from their late cruel despoilers.

Our advance was rapid, and I only had time to stop at Newtown long enough to take supper with dear old Aunt Mary and family.

We had several skirmishes with the enemy on our way; captured quite a number of prisoners and a considerable quantity of army supplies; crossed the

Potomac about July the 5ᵗʰ, 1864; fought and defeated General Lew Wallace, at Monocacy on the ninth, and encamped in front of Washington city and skirmished with the garrison there on the eleventh and twelfth. Here the writer, who had kept his Enfield in reach, exchanged, as did some of his comrades, several shots with the enemy's sharpshooters, who occupied their outworks. This we did more for the purpose of being later able to tell of it than because of any present expectation that our shots would prove generally effective; for certainly no sane man—officer or private—then present or cognizant of the facts, entertained any idea that an actual attack was contemplated, or could possibly be successful if made. Early's army, all told, did not exceed 10,000 effective men. He could not have concentrated, and advanced to attack, until the thirteenth, at which date the enemy could have held the city with, at least, double his numbers; while an enemy army much larger than his own was assembling on his only line of retreat, in the lower valley of Virginia. General Early's chief of artillery, General Long, in his Memoirs of General Lee, when speaking on this subject, says, "The erroneous opinion that the city of Washington should have been taken . . . may be passed over as one of the absurdities of public criticism on the conduct of the war." Undoubtedly, this is a correct exposition of the situation, which no honest historian who knows the facts will gainsay. To us, who were there, it presents the truth as we then understood it.

The rear-guard of our army, of which a detail from our company, in charge of the writer, formed a part, left Washington early on the morning of the thirteenth, passed through Rockville about noon, was relieved a short distance west of that place, and joined the rest of our company, farther on, where it was resting by the road-side.

We had been on duty since midnight, had been skirmishing with the enemy's van all morning, and were now glad to lie down and rest among our comrades. Very soon, however, those of our company who had not been on duty earlier in the day were ordered back to the support of our rear-guard, which now seemed to be rapidly retiring before the enemy's increased numbers. One of my comrades took with him the belt which held my saber and two navy revolvers. A few minutes later, we who had been left behind, were ordered to re-mount, return and join in a charge against the oncoming foe. Unarmed I went with the rest. I was riding a swift, high-spirited mare and soon overtook our comrades in front, and together we all made the charge.

The weather was hot and dry, and the dust on the road must have been nearly half an inch deep. As we neared them, the enemy turned and ran. We struck their rearmost files just as we crossed a small drain, beyond which the dust arose and settled so thick upon us that, even at first, it was almost impossible to distinguish the color of anyone's clothing. Except when we first started on the run there was little or no firing. My speedy mare quickly carried me among and past several of those whom I could dimly see were dressed in blue who halted when ordered; but later we—the mare and I—passed several other dim forms the color of whose clothing I could not certainly tell. And so I rode back nearly to Rockville.

Here I came to firmer roads, resulting in a partially clarified atmosphere, through which I could see that we were practically surrounded by blue-coated riders. This occurred near where a lane or street, coming in from the south, intersected the road upon which we were riding. The situation was not promising, but that lane afforded a possible avenue of escape, of which I took quick advantage; but as, from the dust behind us, I emerged into it, I discovered, a short distance ahead and riding toward me, two men who were unquestionably wearing the blue. Prompt action of some kind was necessary, and almost intuitively, and certainly immediately, it occurred to me that possibly these men had not yet learned whose troops were marching in the dust out of which we had just come; therefore I rode rapidly toward them, calling on them to surrender, and as they turned and ran I followed at top speed yelling "Halt! Halt!" at every bound; all the time feeling that there was less danger in front than from the rear. One of them was especially well mounted; but still my noble mare, in a final spurt, gained rapidly on both, and they abandoned their horses, climbed the lane fence, and made for the wooded hill a short distance away. I reached the one nearest to me just as he started from the opposite side of the fence and, with a threat to shoot, again called on them to halt. He did so but the other ran on. I then ordered the one who had surrendered to hand me the loaded pistol which he still held in his hand, and kept my own empty right hand concealed behind my mare until he complied with my demand. When that Yankee discovered that I had been unarmed, he applied several "cuss-words" to himself. Then, as directed, he handed me the pistol left by the other man in the holster to his saddle; threw down the fence in the direction I wished to return; mounted his own and led the other horse, and moved on before me. Just then rapid firing again broke out near the mouth of the lane which we had entered, and we later learned that my comrades had never quite reached it on that wild charge. Traveling parallel to the road upon which we had charged, I found our command, now supported by our infantry, near the place from which we started. Here I learned that I had been reported killed or captured. My personal trophies consisted of one Yankee, two horses—one of them a splendid animal—well and fully rigged, two navy revolvers and a pair of nice spurs, one of which is still owned by my family. Our charge netted us some forty armed prisoners and nearly as many fully equipped horses. Never again was I caught in an emergency without my belted arms.

We recrossed the Potomac at White's Ford on the 14th of July, and bivouacked for the next two days east of the Blue Ridge. Here my beautiful mare, who had been ailing ever since we made our dusty charge, and whom I had learned to admire and like almost as a human comrade, paid with her life for the splendid temerity she had so willingly shown on that eventful day. I had favored her all I could by placing her in care of our veterinarian, and myself riding the better horse I had just captured. But all proved unavailing, and she died on the night of the fifteenth. The regret I felt at her death was certainly due her, for she had borne me on many fields gallantly and well.

CHAPTER XXXI

BATTLE OF CARTER'S FARM OR STEPHENSON'S DEPOT [RUTHERFORD'S FARM]

MY MOST INTERESTING WAR HOURS
BATTLE OF KERNSTOWN

From Washington we returned to the Shenandoah Valley through Snicker's Gap in the Blue Ridge, on July 16, 1864, and took position on the Shenandoah River. Here our brigade took part in General Early's several successful battles fought at and near Snicker's and Berry's Ferries on the seventeenth, eighteenth and nineteenth. On the morning of the twentieth, a part of our brigade, with a detachment from that of Vaughn—both quite small—were skirmishing with and retreating before General Averell's command, on the Valley Pike, south of Bunker Hill, and continued to do so until we reached Carter's farm. Averell's route would throw him in rear of General Early at Berryville; and General Ramseur's small division had been sent to check, if possible, his advance and was now approaching Carter's farm from the south. From some source Ramseur had learned—or thought he had—that Averell's force was quite small, a fact of which the writer was informed. Therefore, when from an eminence we discovered that he was advancing with a large force composed of all arms, we sent that information, as did the commander of Vaughn's detachment, by couriers back to Ramseur at once; but for some reason he did not, until a fatal lapse of time, act upon it. His failure to do so was, at the time, unknown to us; and our detachment, at least, continued to skirmish with and retreat before the enemy, until they retired their skirmishers, deployed and advanced their two leading regiments in battle-line, and opened with some ten or twelve pieces of artillery upon Ramseur's battery of some three or four pieces, which had just appeared in the Carter woods, less than half a mile away. The ground between was nearly—possibly quite—level and the cannon balls seasoned by those from the small arms—all flying very low—from both sides, made our position so uncomfortable that we felt justified in increasing our pace just a little, so as not to attract too much attention from on-lookers. Before reaching our men the [writer] had dismounted in order to give those balls more room to pass over him. By the time I reached our battery and the very few men supporting it, it had been practically destroyed, and had not enough horses left alive to remove it in any event. I here first heard a horse scream. It was a hideous and piteous cry. He had been shot through both hips with a small cannon ball, and uttered that awful shriek as he fell.

We found that General Ramseur had advanced in column, without skirmishers, until within a short distance of this artillery, and that he was now trying to deploy that column into a battle-line. He was too late. The enemy were among us and had already captured our artillery and a number of our men, and were now advancing with their six regiments, all deployed in line of battle across our front and on our flanks, and we had no choice but to retreat as rapidly, and with as little additional loss as possible; and we hesitated not upon the manner of our going. This situation was then and thereafter known as "Ramseur's Butt." He was, however, a brave and skillful officer, and three months later, on the Cedar Creek battle-field, sealed with his life his devotion to his country and her cause. His error here was the result of misinformation, too readily believed and credulously adhered to.

Even so, we had not retreated far until he had succeeded in throwing out skirmishers on our right (I do not know what took place on our left), and a detachment from our brigade composed entirely, I think, of men from our company and from Captain Marshall's was, for the purpose of protecting their right flank, ordered out on a road running parallel to, and a short distance in rear of, their line. With Marshall's men leading, we were only well on our way, when the enemy's cavalry, in a curved line extending beyond the right of our skirmishers, as well as our own, and in strong force, charged over the rise in our front, occupied by our men, who were wholly unable to stop them. It was a situation requiring immediate action; and our gallant Major Lady, ordered us to dismount and open fire upon them. To do so would not only endanger the lives of our comrades, among whom the enemy were already intermingling and making prisoners, but in the end would avail us nothing. There was a low fence in our front and, without waiting to reason with the Major, we went over and through it and at those Yankees on a dead run, determined to do or die. Just as we started on our way, glancing to our right, the writer saw Lieutenant J. G. Ward, of Captain Marshall's Company, followed by most of his men, dash over or through that fence and forward, apparently vying with us in the race as to who should first reach the exultant enemy. My Yankee horse proved to be as speedy as the best, and we were among them almost before they knew of our coming. Our charge was eminently successful, we not only released most of our temporarily captured comrades, but sent them back in charge of many of their recent captors. Our maneuver had isolated some of the enemy who had reached the road, upon which we had been advancing, beyond the place at which we had left it; and some of us now went in pursuit of and, for some distance, engaged in a running fight with them. It was here that our gallant comrade, Jacob Salisbury, was killed by one of the enemy who had previously surrendered. His treacherous foe did not live long enough to boast of his act.

This charge, in addition to releasing many of our men, netted us some thirty unwounded Federal prisoners, with most of their horses, and effectually stopped General Averell's advance for the time. Returning to our command, the writer found Major Lady reporting him to General

Jackson for disobedience to orders. The General who occasionally "swore a few" waited patiently until the Major finished his complaint, and then, with a sly but unmistakable wink at me, said, "Well! Well! Major, it appears to have been a damned disorderly proceeding, but it was the damnedest best thing that ever happened and we will let it pass."

While Carman, in giving his account of this battle in the Americana, admits that Jackson's men halted those of Averell on this occasion, yet, among other errors, he says that we only captured six prisoners, when the fact was that we captured about five times that number.

In order to cover all the roads by which the enemy were advancing from the lower Valley, General Early had, on the 22nd of July, 1864, concentrated his army at Cedar Creek. About the same time the Federal army under General Crook had assembled at Kernstown; and on the twenty-third we started after him, arrived near his position late in the evening and halted for the night. I had been on duty for the last twenty-four hours, had all that afternoon been skirmishing with the enemy's rear, on the road leading along near the eastern base of Little North Mountain, and had just lain down to rest near General Jackson's bivouac, when one of his messengers appeared and said the General wanted to see me. I went at once and found that a detachment, to be commanded by Major Stewart and guided by Dick Johnson (with both of whom I was then unacquainted), was being formed for the purpose of carrying a dispatch to our General Vaughn, who was supposed to be in the vicinity of Bartonsville on the pike. It was known that when a boy I had resided for some time both at Stephenson's Depot and Newtown, was tolerably well acquainted with the country between those points, and had for two seasons worked in the harvest fields at Bartonsville; and the General now requested me to go, as an additional guide, with the detail; but, knowing of the arduous service from which I had just been relieved, added that I need not return with it, nor until such time as I chose, and left both my going and returning optional with myself.

I went, my most interesting forty eight war-hours commenced to run, and I shall now tell just what occurred therein. We reached the pike through a large unfenced field bordering thereon about midway between Bartonsville and Kernstown, and just south of where Joe Barton, with whom I had harvested, then resided. We paused for a few moments. All was quiet. It was impossible for us to know whether or not we were on "No man's land," or who was to the right or left of us. We dismounted on the grass on our side of the pike; and on foot I proceeded northward along it some twenty-five or thirty yards, where I reached Joe's yard gate on my left, and, entering it, passed to a door in the rear part of his house, which opened to the south. Within the house darkness ruled. Again I paused and listened. Except for the rustling of the night-wind, as it swept through the tree-tops in the forest we had just left behind us, and through the foliage of the shrubbery around me, all was still. I tapped on the door. Joe must have been awake for, although he appeared in dishabille, he immediately opened it and recognized me. Naturally he was surprised and somewhat excited; but, as rapidly as possible, told me: that none of our men had yet passed his house; that a small detail of Federal cavalry had gone up towards Bartonsville just at night-fall; that he had not heard them return, but that they might have done so; that the Federal army was in position near Kernstown about a mile to the north; and that their infantry picket was posted on the pike, less than three hundred yards from the northeast corner of his yard fence, at which their advance sentinels were stationed.

As I returned I verified what he had told me about these sentinels—there appeared to be several of them—and then hastily rejoined my comrades and reported. The Major was inclined to abandon our expedition, but some others insisted that we proceed on our way, and it was finally determined that, with Dick and me leading, followed a short distance behind by the others—first on the grass and then on the pike—we should move on toward Bartonsville. In the manner and direction named, we advanced about one-fourth of a mile, and were approaching the top of a low ridge, when a small detachment of cavalry appeared on its crest. Both parties came to an immediate halt, and each inquired of the other who they were. We were below and in the dark; they above and in the light. This gave us some advantage, both as to accurate shooting and the ascertainment of opposing numbers. The distance between us must have been less than thirty yards, but a moderate wind was passing eastward. When called upon, as to who we were, I told them, as distinctly as possible, that we were couriers from General Jackson carrying a dispatch to General Vaughn. The reply was an order to fire, the flash of several pistols or carbines, and the singing overhead of considerable wasted lead. The flash-light from that volley was so near to, and vivid in, the faces of our horses—Dick's and mine—that they reversed ends. As we again faced them I repeated my former statement, to which they apparently listened for they did not again shoot until I had ended. Then their former reply, as well as the action of our horses, was duplicated. In the meantime we had learned, from the noise it made, that our support had left the pike and retired to the edge of the woods through which we came, and now Dick's horse followed them, My own hat had been carried off, either by a disremembered dodge, the wind, or the enemy's bullets. Their actions, so far, rendered me almost certain that they were our own men, and looking back at the situation now, I am inclined to think that, as alone I faced them for the third time, I was more angry than scared, but doubtless I was both. I had not yet fired a shot, but now, after again telling them who I was and what my object, added that "we" would do so, if they continued to shoot. Their answer, in lesser volume, was the same; and uttering a feeble Confederate yell, and firing a shot or two intended to go over their heads, I rode rapidly toward them, keeping, however, on the safe side of the pike. They retired. I was of the opinion then, and am yet, that they did so because of my apparent flank movement and their uncertain knowledge as to what force was concealed by the darkness behind me—something I had largely depended upon. I now went to the position from which they had been firing upon us and from there could see the campfires at Bartonsville, which were necessarily, those of our own men.

After spending a few minutes in unsuccessfully looking for my hat, I sought and joined my comrades at the edge of the woods to which they had retired, and reported the certainty that we were facing our men and not the enemy; but the Major was still inclined to return to camp with our mission unfulfilled. We refused to do so and it was then agreed that we should proceed by a trail, with which I was acquainted, to a road leading into Bartonsville from the west. A comrade furnished me with a hat and we went. When we reached the road, I was so certain that our only trouble would be in passing our own pickets that I went on ahead whistling Dixie; and had gone but a short distance when halted by a sentinel. I stopped and asked what he wanted. He ordered me to dismount, advance and give the countersign. I told him I had no countersign to give, that I was a Confederate soldier, that I was carrying my pistol in my hand, was going to advance and would shoot him if [he was] a Yankee and shake hands, if a rebel. He laughed and spoke to some one who called to me to come on. I went and found some of General Johnson's (not Vaughn's as we expected) men who knew me. They passed us on and our trouble ended. Major Stewart reported to General Johnson, left me with him and returned. The general had my horse taken care of and myself furnished with a late supper and a blanketed floor on which to sleep. Just before I retired a cavalry captain appeared and reported to the General that some distance northward on the pike, he had met, skirmished with and driven back a detachment of the enemy's cavalry. From what he said it was impossible not to recognize him as the commander of the squad with whom we had just been skirmishing. Upon being questioned he admitted he heard what I said about having a dispatch for Vaughn, and that the entire incident was just as above given, but, as a partial excuse, claimed he was misled to some extent, because we said we were seeking Vaughn instead of Johnson. The General, who did not always use pious language, now, in his vehement denunciation of the Captain, used a vast amount of the other kind. He threatened to have the poor fellow cashiered and continued to abuse him until I interceded in his behalf and he was allowed to leave with his rank.

In the early dawn of the next morning, I reached our battle-ground of the preceding night, and took in the scene before me. The Federal sentinels, several in number, still stood at the corner of Barton's yard fence; but they had moved up a line of cavalry videttes, which was now stretched across the pike just south of his house. My hat was lying some fifty feet from the place where I had lost it, carried there I suppose by the wind. I rode to where it was lying, stooped and picked it up without leaving my saddle, and turned back. When I did so some of those videttes on and near the pike trotted toward me, but when I halted and turned, fell back to their line. I had no rifle or carbine with me and I do not suppose they had. We were not within pistol range. I found my hat, which had previously suffered a good deal from wear and tear, very much dilapidated; enough so to lend some color to the claim made that it had been victimized by Yankee bullets; a claim which the writer, who knew the hat, very much doubted.

Returning to General Johnson's quarters, my horse and I breakfasted and again moved forward to the hilltop where we had skirmished. It was yet early morning. None of our men were in our front on the pike. The enemy's cavalry videttes and infantry pickets had been withdrawn; but their troops, apparently in force, could be seen in the vicinity of Kernstown. In a field to my right, some distance away, and slightly in advance, Major Gilmore's Battalion of cavalry stood in column, facing one of the enemy's of about equal numbers, at some three hundred yards. Some of Gilmore's men had dismounted and were tearing down an intervening stone fence; and it was evident that he was preparing to charge. He and I had frequently met at my aunt's in Newtown, and had often bantered each other as to the relative merits of Maryland and Virginia soldiers. I now rode up to him and said we would test that question, by seeing which would go first and farthest on the present occasion. He told me to wait a moment and I should be accommodated. And let me here say that those Marylanders—especially a boy named Tom Kidd—went far enough in the direction we started, to satisfy the ambition of any one. It certainly did mine. We drove the enemy back until a new column came in on our flank and the Major ordered us to retreat and we did.

He had no sooner placed all our adversaries directly in our rear, than, in a magnificent voice, Gilmore gave the command, "Right about, Charge!"; and we obeyed. I then happened to be slightly behind, consequently was that much in advance when we turned. The enemy were considerably scattered at the time—the best horses ridden by the best riders being in front. Their leader was an officer mounted on a splendidly equipped horse. He fell within fifteen feet of me and his horse ran on. I dropped my empty pistol which was tied to me, and while drawing my sabre, turned and called to Gilmore, who was just a few feet behind, that the horse was mine. He called back, "All right." I turned to the front again, barely in time to catch and deflect with my own, the descending sabre of another gallant foe, whose horse carried him past me on my left. By now the scattered leaders of the enemy were retiring for the purpose of concentration, while those of our own were halting for a like purpose. This apparently isolated the brave fellow, who had gone by me, from his comrades; but unhesitatingly he turned, passed through our still scattered men behind me, and started up a sloping hillside on a bearing inclining toward his own men. War always seemed less of a "Hell" to me when following than when facing my enemies; so I turned and went after him.

Discovering that he would be intercepted and taken at a disadvantage unless he changed his course, he veered ,just enough, as we almost met, to pass in front of me. At first his straight run gave his horse a slight advantage over mine while changing on to his new line of retreat. At that moment a loud cheer from our respective comrades greeted us. I glanced back to see if our skirmish had been renewed. Neither party was advancing. The cheering was for us. From here on our race was almost "nip and tuck," with the writer slowly, very slowly, gaining foot by foot; while the Yankee, without faltering, or halting when ordered, steadfastly watched me over his shoulder. He could not turn to defend himself. It was impossible to safely do so. When we crossed the crest of that hill, some two hundred and fifty yards from our starting point, I could almost reach him with my sabre, and we were so engrossed in the chase that we did not see the left flank of the Federal battle-line, lying there, until within a few paces of it. A way was hastily made for him and he passed through before he could turn. My incentive was greater. I succeeded in turning, without stopping, almost within reach of those infantrymen, retopped, dropped over and went back down that hill so rapidly that the few bullets fired at me passed harmlessly over my head, and caused Gilmore's men to say with some truth, as they did, that if I had gone over it as fast as I came back, I would certainly have caught that Yank. I never again saw the finely equipped horse, as promised by Gilmore. He told me, honestly, I think, that he did not know what became of it. When I called on him for his judgment upon the relative merits of the Maryland and Virginia soldiers, his answer was, "Oh damn it, by birth you are, yourself, a Marylander," which was true.

Our infantry was now approaching, and our skirmish ended by the retirement of all the cavalry engaged in it. Knowing that the men of my old company and regiment were advancing west of the pike with

General Ramseur's division, I now crossed over it, and found and joined them as they moved forward in battle array. They were already in range of the enemy's artillery, planted on the hills at Kernstown about a mile distant, the balls from which were whistling over them. The enemy's battle-line was stationed behind a stone fence near the foot of those hills. No skirmishers now intervened. The boys gave me cheerful greeting and a pressing invitation to go with them—so pressing that, without dismounting, I went. They, as did all their comrades on that line of battle, moved forward unfalteringly and steadily, yelling loudly and firing rapidly, until they reached that stone fence. Then the more agile among our enemies made good their retreat. Others less swift were captured. The writer jumped his horse over the fence in time, with the assistance of others, to stop and capture several of them before they could get started. Just then the rifle balls whistled around, and over, me so thick and close that I glanced to my right to learn the cause of it. I discovered, about a hundred and twenty-five yards distant, stretcher bearers carrying a wounded soldier away on a stretcher; and that it was a group of their gallant comrades, who had formed for their protection in their rear, that had done that unpleasant shooting. They were also now retiring. That was all that I learned at the time; but after the war closed, when discussing this fight and this incident with my old-time friend, Thomas C. Curtis, late of Elkins, who was a Federal soldier present at the time, he at once recognized the situation, told me the color of the horse I was riding, said he was one of the group mentioned and that it was the mortally wounded Colonel Mulligan lying on the stretcher, and that because I was mounted he, and others he named, commenced shooting at me, even before coming over the fence. Tom was unequivocally glad that he had missed me, but always appeared to be a little ashamed of his bad shooting. He died as he had lived, my warm friend.

Our loss at Kernstown was, as compared with that of the enemy, remarkably small. Our men stopped a few moments at that fence to adjust their alignment and dispose of their prisoners. While they were doing so, I started on. Just then a mounted officer—General Lomax I think—with a small escort, rode up and went with me. He must have inquired who I was, for he addressed me by name and rank. We started from near the left of our battle-line, but, in order to avoid going over the vacated hill in our front, still inclined to our left. We had gone but a short distance when we saw one of the enemy, to our left front, riding up through a half fenced field, apparently lost. Promising the General to return and guide him, I went after that blue-coat. At first I thought he was alone but soon discovered that he was following some of his comrades who had gone into the woods, through a gap in the fence, near the top of the hill. I gained rapidly and was near him when he entered the woods. Just then I heard a noise to my left and nearby; and glancing in that direction saw Captain Hutton mounted on his horse, Stonewall, riding at top speed, almost parallel to, and even with me. I called to know where he was going. Without pausing his only answer was, "Did you see that damned Yank go through that gap?" Side by side we now passed through it, over the rise in the hill beyond and into a group of about a dozen bewildered Yankees—some still mounted, and others standing beside their horses—who appeared to be completely lost and who surrendered at once; the more readily, perhaps, because of the near approach of some of Hutton's men, who now advanced and took charge of them.

After an absence of less than fifteen minutes, and carrying with me, as a trophy of our recent success, a Spencer carbine, I rejoined the General and we moved on in the direction of and nearly to, Winchester. Here we skirmished with a detachment of the enemy which we found on a hillock to our left. They retreated and I followed them, but the General and his escort left me and rode on to Winchester. Upon reaching the hilltop I found that the detachment mentioned had consisted of dismounted cavalry, who were now mounted and rapidly retreating.

With slight effect I tried to hurry them on with my captured carbine. I could have done better with my old Enfield. Moving on I discovered, at the place where these men had mounted, a considerable quantity of food and forage, and a number of the finest India rubber blankets I had ever seen. My horse and I accepted those eatables as a perfect godsend and proceeded to place ourselves outside enough of them to sustain our lives for the next twenty four hours, should that become necessary; taking the precaution, however, to carry some of them, as well as several of those splendid blankets with us. Both my horse and I had been slightly wounded in this last skirmish—so slightly that it did not affect our appetites.

I now hastened on my way, overtook some of our cavalrymen just after they had crossed the Romney pike west of Winchester, and soon thereafter joined them in a skirmish with the enemy. I was struck on the thigh and somewhat bruised, by a half-spent rifle ball, but upon the retreat of the Yankees continued to ride with our men until reaching the pike, some distance south of Stephenson's Depot, where the advance of our main army had halted for the night. I then rode forward to our advanced picket. It was composed of some of General Johnson's men, whom I knew; and was stationed within half a mile of where the road leading westward to my boyhood's home left the pike, with its advanced sentinels half-way between. With their knowledge I rode on to that road, paused, and for some time listened and quietly waited. It was now after 10 o'clock. Darkness enveloped me and the rain was falling heavily. Otherwise all was still and quiet. Near where I stood, a dilapidated rail fence ran westward from the pike along the edge of a woods, and following it a few paces, I dismounted, hitched my horse to one of its inside corners, spread one of my captured blankets on the ground nearby, lay down and covered myself with another, and so rested. The situation was wholly novel, but not unpleasant, and to the lullaby sung by the rain as it fell upon, around and over me, I soon fell sound asleep, and awoke not until the twittering of the birds, nesting in the oaken branches above me, announced the coming dawn. The rain had ceased to fall, and the morning zephyrs seemed to whisper, "All is well," but it was not. Before it was fully light, my horse and I had breakfasted on our captured food, and refreshed by our quiet rest, were ready for the day's work. It was also ready for us, for with the coming of daylight, I discovered the enemy's pickets standing in the pike, not over two hundred yards distant and, at once, commenced exchanging shots with them. They retreated as General Johnson's men arrived. We pursued, and continued to pursue, them throughout the day, having many skirmishes with them on our way. Those at Bunker Hill, Darksville and Martinsburg arising almost to the dignity of battles. Our infantry did not arrive in time to take any considerable part in any of them. As we advanced, we captured a number of prisoners and a quantity of army supplies and equipment, including many wagons—some loaded, some empty and others half burnt. At one time, being slightly ahead and following a turn in the pike, I saw a Yankee setting fire to a wagon, about seventy five yards distant, and rode rapidly at him, shooting as I went. He had just dropped a bundle of blazing hay in it, but now took to the adjacent woods without his horse. Paying but little further attention to him, I jumped into the wagon and saved it by throwing out the burning hay. Just then a ball, shot by one of our own men, who did not know I was ahead, and who supposed I was a Yankee, whizzed past me. He was preparing to shoot again when a few profane words from General Johnson stopped him. The General seemed to think—and I likewise—that the situation was such an incentive thereto, that the use of such words was excusable. The man's apologies were heartfelt.

When approaching the outskirts of Martinsburg, General Jackson's brigade rode up, and I joined my Company. We now made a successful charge which was led by our company and Captain Marshall's, and bivouacked on the ground won on the road side near the town. Somewhat tired, but satisfied, I rested, and slept soundly throughout the following night.

Undoubtedly the pleasure, if any I had, growing out of my preceding forty eight war-hours, was greatly enhanced by the fact that, most of the time, I had been facing the Yankees going instead of coming. A situation which I always highly appreciated.

French Harding
Taken from postcard
(no date)

CHAPTER XXXII

CEDAR CREEK—WINCHESTER— SHEPHERDSTOWN—SMITHFIELD

The writer is not certain as to the exact sequence of the military events occurring between the rival armies in the Shenandoah Valley, from late in July until nearly the middle of August, 1864; but he distinctly remembers that at the time he considered them fully as onerous as glorious.

After capturing Martinsburg, we remained near there, Bunker Hill, and Winchester until about the 10th of August. During that period the writer was almost continually on duty—most of the time scouting. On several occasions D. D. Dix, a fifteen-year-old relative of General Stonewall Jackson, whose gallantry in our recent charge at Martinsburg first attracted my attention, and whom we called "Dixie," accompanied me and proved to be a splendid companion. One night in the vicinity of Lee Town, we came so near running into a detachment of Federals, known as the "Dixie Boys," who dressed in gray and infested that section, that we all took supper at the same table from which the residue of the eatables had not been removed between the meals; but notwithstanding we saw and heard them near-by, yet, with the aid of one of the younger ladies of the house, who apparently became interested in Dixie, we obtained the important information we sought, and safely returned to camp. At another time when scouting in the direction of Berryville with two or three of our comrades, we called at a house standing a short distance from the road, from which we saw a detachment of the enemy ride, in order, if possible, to learn their intentions. We obtained the knowledge we wanted, but when we undertook to return the way we came, found ourselves cut off and almost surrounded by the Yankees. Of course we had more of a run than a fight for it, but again got safely away with the information we went for, and with less damage than we inflicted. And so the period named was filled with as many, or more, like incidents than it numbered days.

About August the tenth, General Sheridan, who had then taken command of the Federal forces in the Valley, moved them from Hall Town by the way of Berryville, southward. In order to cover all the roads leading from the north, General Early fell back behind Cedar Creek. Captain Hutton was at that time temporarily absent on detached service. Our company, in charge of the writer, independently filled a section of the rear-guard skirmish line to our army. The van of General Sheridan's advancing army was composed of a heavy skirmish line of infantry or dismounted cavalry, supported by cavalry advancing in column. To prevent capture in case we were compelled to hastily retreat, which, on account of the paucity of our numbers as compared with theirs, appeared to be imminent, we kept our horses near-by; but I adopted the plan of dismounting half of our men in a good position and sending the other half, with all our horses, a short distance back to select another such position and await our coming. Alternating the men, we repeated this maneuver several times, with the result that the enemy's line, both to our right and left, advanced more rapidly than in our front, thereby giving us considerable trouble, which we, to some extent, mitigated by occasionally giving them a flank fire. At last they halted, and several of our officers, who had witnessed our leisurely retirement, rode up and congratulated us upon the manner of its making.

A day or two later, General Early started rapidly back after General Sheridan, and the latter at once, and as rapidly, commenced to retreat. It would be difficult to determine why. His army must have numbered over twice that of ours. His splendidly equipped cavalry numbered nearly, possibly quite, as many as our entire army. His action may be accounted for by the fact that he had been, and still was, copying after the example of Hunter, who had desolated the upper Valley, and had inherited the latter's conscience. We overtook and charged his cavalry at Winchester—Randolph boys led the charge on one of its streets. The enemy precipitately abandoned the town, nor halted until they joined their main army at Berryville; and even there their stand was short and unsuccessful. With heavy loss in men, material and prestige, Sheridan continued to retreat until reaching Hall Town from whence he had started. Here we faced and skirmished with his men for a few days; and here the following incident occurred:

One day the men of my old infantry company were skirmishing in front of where our cavalry was stationed and, strolling forward to see how they were faring, I found them facing the enemy's skirmishers, who occupied a superior position on a wooded hillside some three hundred yards distant. One of them had taken position behind a large tree slightly in advance of their main line, and was giving our men considerable trouble. Owing to the formation of the ground to our left-front, my old comrade, Jack Apperson, had safely approached and was now lying behind a stump about one hundred yards from him; but his tree was so large that he could shield himself from Jack, behind it, without exposing his person to any of our men on the other side. To our right-front a peach orchard, filled with young trees, extended for some distance. Since our return from Washington, Levi Heavener, of my old company, had been carrying my Enfield most of the time. I now took it, informed Jack of my intentions, told him to hold himself ready to shoot when he heard from me, crept through that orchard until I could see, some two hundred yards to my left-front, a line of blue bordering that tree; and, although the mark was small, when my Enfield spoke, the bark flew and the blue disappeared, Jack's gun answered and that gallant soldier's troubles, as well as ours growing out of his gallantry, had ended. Truly Sherman was right—"War is Hell."

So far as I can now remember, this was the last shot I made with that reliable old Enfield.

On the 25th of August, leaving part of our army still facing General Sheridan at Hall Town, we marched toward Shepherdstown. In the mean time I had developed a severe case of boils; and had also traded my Rockville mount for another swift but rough-gaited Yankee horse. These two things, especially because of the location of some of those boils, were not conducive to comfortable horse-back riding. Indeed they made it painfully uncomfortable; and our doctor directed me to remain in the rear with our hospital corps but I stayed near my company and made my way in the easiest manner possible. Most of our cavalry crossed the Potomac to Williamsport; part of our infantry advanced upon and defeated a force of the enemy somewhere northeast of Lee Town, and late in the afternoon our brigade met and engaged that of General Custer—or possibly only part of it and part of another acting therewith—near, and on a road leading into, Shepherdstown. After a brief skirmish, our men were ordered to charge. We were close-by when they did so, and the yell they raised when they started was too much for the equanimity of my war-horse. He went rapidly after them and, of course, willy-nilly, I went with him. When we struck their line the shock seemed to sever it, and they retreated in different directions on different roads. I was not very well acquainted with Shepherdstown, but as I remember it part of our regiment, led by some of the best mounted in our company, charged through it on a street running in a south-eastern direction. The enemy apparently sought to escape by turning to the left toward the river, as opportunity offered. There was but little fighting. We picked up a few prisoners on the way. My horse proved fully as swift as Captain Hutton's Stonewall. As we neared the southern boundary of the town, we overtook, and after a melee, captured a squad of the enemy. The pause made enabled their now scattered leaders to get a considerable start, and, leaving the Captain to dispose of our prisoners, I rode on after them.

Upon leaving the outskirts of the town, I discovered to my right, and not over one hundred and fifty yards distant, a detachment of the enemy, apparently composed of both infantry and cavalry, moving in column in a direction that would lead them across the road we were on about the same distance ahead of me. A fence and some shrubbery partly concealed me from them. The head of their column was already nearing the road. I had some trouble in checking my horse, but did so as quickly as possible, dismounted, took position at the fence, and commenced using my Spencer. This all happened in a few moments. Just then the Captain, with his eyes fixed upon some of the now distant enemy with whom we had been engaged, riding up the hills to our left, dashed up, and had well nigh passed me before I could get his attention fixed upon that near-by column, which was already crossing the road. He dismounted at once, and added to their haste. He had not been aware of the presence of the detachment of the enemy mentioned, until I stopped him, and always claimed that I had saved him from death or capture, which was probably true for he was rashly brave.

The enemy continued to retreat; we followed rapidly, skirmishing as we advanced, and closed the day with a little battle across the Potomac, on the north bank of which they made a stand. Here our lieutenant, James McLaughlin, who on account of ill health, had not been with us before during the campaign, received a slight wound from which he later died. Early next morning we returned to Shepherdstown. Captain Hutton and I were standing on the street in front of General Jackson's quarters when he came out with his pistol in his hand. He walked to his horse, undertook to place the revolver in the holster attached to the saddle, but missing it caught the hammer of his pistol on its side, discharging it, thereby shooting himself. We assisted him to his room and helped the doctor examine and dress his wound, which was slight. He swore a few and soon got well. General Early gathered his now scattered army together and retired toward Smithfield and Bunker Hill. No one but myself knows how all this time those boils had been, and still were, hurting me.

On the night of the 27th of August, our regiment, now very small, bivouacked a short distance north of Smithfield, and early next morning moved toward Lee Town. Before reaching that place, fighting between the Federals, under General Merritt, and our men, under General Fitzhugh Lee, had commenced. On account of the enemy's numerical superiority, Lee was compelled to retreat. I do not remember what he later did or where he went; but do distinctly remember that it was not long until our little band, with some of Gilmore's men, were facing General Merritt's men in our front, alone; and saw that he was leading the largest body of cavalry we had ever seen together on any field of battle. We, however continued to make a running fight of it, and while facing him made several charges upon the head of his advancing host. The last charge we so made took place but a short distance north of Smithfield. Here the enemy furiously charged us in return and we had to run. This occurred when we were about three hundred yards from some fenced fields traversed by a lane opening into the road on which we were retreating and leading into Smithfield. Captain Hutton rode to my right and slightly in advance. Just then I distinctly heard the impact of a bullet that struck him, saw him wilt in his saddle and start to fall toward me. His motion slightly checked the speed of his horse, thus enabling me to catch him as he fell and straighten him up on his saddle, at the same time enquiring where he had been hit. Raising his hand to the right side of his face he answered, "That damned Yankee shot the whole side of my head off." No doubt it so felt to him, for the bullet had passed through his ear so near to his head that it bruised it, and still left the outside of the ear untouched. As he rode on for the mouth of that lane, his grin was rather sickly, but he safely reached it and made his escape.[*]

---

[*] This incident is mentioned in M. P. H. Potts' *A Boy Scout of The Confederacy* (1923).

By now the enemy both from right and left were closing in upon and mingling with our men, and a regular melee resulted. Among other happenings, I saw to my left, and about fifty yards from the mouth of the lane, for which he was riding, my company comrade, Andrew Ware, and meeting him with drawn sabre, one of the enemy who had passed us. Andy was a physical giant, but now had nothing but an empty rifle with which to defend himself. A few loads yet remained in one of my pistols, and I tried to reach him before his enemy could, but failed; and as they met the sabre-stroke of the one rung out on the gun-barrel of the other. The gun fell to the ground, but, instantly, the sabre-handle was in Andy's grasp and the return stroke he made with it, effectually, and for all time, settled the dispute. It all occurred so rapidly that the motions made were not all observable. All I know is that it so happened. With the few shots remaining in my pistol, I aided Andy in safely entering the mouth of the lane. Some of the enemy had already entered it and gone on. Three of Gilmore's men, among them my friend Tom Kidd, entered it from the opposite side of the road, just as a few of the enemy and I did. My sabre was now in my hand, but fortunately Gilmore's men had not yet entirely emptied their pistols. One of the enemy as he entered the lane slightly in advance of us, whirled and ordered us to surrender, and dropped his cocked pistol within a foot of my breast. By this time I was striking at him with my sabre, and instead of shooting, or if he tried to shoot his pistol must have snapped, he, in an effort to avoid my sabre-stroke which he partly did, reined his horse back almost on his haunches, and before he could recover, if recovery was possible, or I could withdraw my sabre point from the pommel of his saddle in which it was buried, three bullets from the weapons fired by Gilmore's men passed through his body and so he bravely died.* We now moved on with some of the enemy before, and others behind us. Few

---

* Part of this incident is also mentioned in *A Boy Scout of The Confederacy*, page 20.

could shoot without endangering the lives of friends. None would stop, so long as the enemy in our rear pursued us; and so we rode until we passed through a line of our dismounted men, and the incident, so far as we were concerned, ended with the capture of the twelve or fifteen foemen ahead of us, and the repulse of the many behind us. Of what took place between our forces, later that evening, or in the next few days, I cannot speak with certainty. We were moved some distance toward Bunker Hill and bivouacked. Although somewhat bruised and battered, we were "still in the ring."

The writer was so tormented by those boils, by his painfully sprained wrist, the result of the contact of his sabre-point with that saddle-pommel, and by other excoriations and hurts; that he was not only inclined to look upon war as a "Hell" generally, but as one applicable to himself, personally. Our doctor now ordered me to retire to some hospital in our rear. I was not in love with hospitals, and trouble ensued. It was compromised, and I was furnished a front-line ambulance in which to ride. No braver man than its driver ever lived.

About this time a controversy as to the true ownership of my rough-gaited horse arose between the man who had traded him to me and another claimant; and I turned him over to the disputants, and saw him no more. I had other horses but none so swift or rough as he.

CHAPTER XXXIII

DEATH OF LIEUTENANT GENE HUTTON—OUR LAST ADVANCE ON MARTINSBURG—BATTLES OF WINCHESTER AND FISHER'S HILL

Early on the morning of the 3rd of September, our brigade was retreating before the overwhelming force of the enemy just south of Bunker Hill. Our company, under the immediate command of Lieutenant Gene Hutton, was on our line west of, and next to, the pike. The gallant driver of my ambulance kept on the line, in the pike. This gave me a rest for the muzzle of my gun when shooting at the enemy following us. I could see my company comrades, as they slowly retired, frequently stop and return the fire of the oncoming foe. In this manner we retreated for some time and had reached the edge of a woods. It was here I last saw Gene alive. He was preparing to make another stand as he entered, and was hid from me by the woods, about fifty yards from where I was riding in my ambulance. The enemy following us made but a little pause and our retreat continued. We had driven on but a short distance when one of our men came out from the woods and told me Gene had been killed. Determined to succor him if he retained a spark of life, or to recover his body if not, I left the ambulance, and with the few, but willing, men around me opened a more vigorous fire upon the enemy and started back. Most likely we would have failed in our purpose, but just then General Rodes' division of infantry appeared and our foes hastily retreated. When we reached Gene he was dead. His death had been instantaneous. He was lying on his face with one of his pistols in his hand under him. The enemy had overlooked it but had taken the other. Among all those of the South-land, who fought and bled for it to uphold a principle we all revered, there fell no manlier, truer, more gallant, or more conscientious man than he. In him the South lost one of her bravest and best sons and his soldier comrades a glorious leader, who never asked them to go where he would not lead. While all those with whom I was closely associated in the army proved friends tried and true, yet, after the death of my brothers, Gene became my special chum and, as near as possible, filled the void they left with me.

I already had complete control of the movements of myself and ambulance, but took pains to get special permission from our division commander, General Lomax, to convey my comrade's remains to Newtown, for burial. His brother, our recently wounded captain, had not yet returned to us. Three of Gene's soldier friends assisted in placing him in the ambulance, and one of them, A. C. Crouch, accompanied me to Newtown, where we stopped at my aunt's. Several friends, both of his and ours, came, bringing many beautiful flowers, and remained with us throughout the night. On the next day, in a very plain but substantial coffin, and with impressively appropriate services, we buried him in the Lutheran grave-yard in that town. There he peacefully slept until 1905, when we brought him home and laid him in the Brick Church Cemetery, near Huttonsville. There, after a rightly spent life, consummated by a glorious death, he still rests well.

Returning at once to our army, we found our division still camped near Bunker Hill. Disregarding the doctor's orders, I now abandoned the ambulance, bid its brave driver goodbye, joined and remained with my company during the rest of the 1864 Valley Campaign; but was compelled, at first, to move slowly and carefully. The hurts received at Smithfield proved worse than even the doctor thought them at the time, but soon got well.

And now from the 8th to the 18th of September, I resumed my scouting life; accompanied, alternately by "Dixie," Tom Kidd, and Dick Johnson—all good comrades; and we had several unimportant skirmishes; several narrow escapes; several rapid retreats, but, withal, usually returned to our command with the information sought. At that time I was the only officer with my company.

On the morning of the 18th of September, General Lomax's cavalry was fronted by that of General Averell at Martinsburg. Our brigade comprised our advanced line. Marshall's Randolph Company was formed in column on the pike, and ours on a road a short distance east of it. Each was to lead the proposed charge on its respective road. We could see the enemy's column passing from east to west through the suburbs of the town. While awaiting orders, several of the boys began to guy me on the looks of my horse, which had recently been brought to me from the rear. He was not specially good-looking, but I had tried him, and found him both swift and plucky. Among those about me were Dixie and a somewhat boastful comrade—not from Randolph. The latter now claimed that he could and would, on his better horse, lead the charge. We started to the music of our customary yell. The distance to go was some four hundred yards. The fire delivered by our leading boys and those of Marshall's company, apparently opened simultaneously. The enemy in our front seemed to be taken by surprise, and we passed through their column without serious loss. Those on our left retreated, pursued by Marshall's men, on the Williamsport road. Those to our right, on the road leading to Shepherdstown. We followed them but they had supports with artillery at the Opequon, which halted before reaching that stream. We dismounted and while preparing to charge on foot, our boasting comrade arrived. He claimed that while his horse kept well up at first, he had failed toward the last. Dixie, who with several others had kept up all the way, and who now appeared to be somewhat suspicious, told him that probably he could do better in the charge we were now going to make on foot. He claimed that none of us could outrun him. Again when he came up from the rear, to where we had halted after dislodging the now retreating foe, Dixie told him that the speed of both himself and horse apparently depended on the direction they were going. Small, but among war's horrors, pleasant things to remember, and they remain with us.

We were now recalled and rejoined the rest of our command in Martinsburg. "Uncle" Jack Baker, a brave but eccentric middle-aged soldier of Marshall's company, who had christened one of his horses Billy Baker and another Betsy Baker, in honor of his wife—I do not know which he was riding at the time—and who was one of the leaders of his company in the charge just made, had had his horse killed by a near-by foe, but had immediately and certainly avenged its death with his sabre.

We now collected the fruits of our victory and hastened to Winchester, where we met the advancing hosts of General Sheridan on the morrow.

The battle of Winchester—sometimes called Opequon—fought on the 19th, and of Fisher's Hill fought on the 22nd of September, both resulted in clear defeats of our army; defeats about which historians favoring the North have, as clearly, misrepresented General Early, and for which those favoring the South who were uninformed or unfriendly have, without reason, adversely criticised him. In each of these battles he was fighting over three to his one, both in men and means. If he made any mistake here at all, it was because he did not avoid them by a timely retreat. Our brigade took an active part in both.

At Winchester, early in the morning, we were dismounted and formed on our battle-line on the right flank of General Ramseur's infantry division, which was already engaged. Very soon we were ordered to charge, and, with the infantry did so, driving back the enemy for some distance. In this charge we captured a few prisoners, and our company took one regimental flag. After holding the position taken from the foe for some time, in which we repulsed a counter charge, a lull in the fighting occurred, and Ramseur's men were moved to the right; thus taking our place, while, still dismounted, we were taken toward the left of his line. While on our way, marching in rear of, and near to his men, they were again attacked by the enemy. We were halted, the enemy repulsed, and a counter attack ordered. It so happened that, just then, we were immediately in rear of my old infantry company. My old-time comrades saw me, called on me to go with them and I went—leaving our brigade resting. The enemy were driven back a short distance, and our line established at the place reached. I then rejoined my own company, and went with it to the position assigned us on Ramseur's left, from which we could plainly see Winchester and the extensive plain west of it. In the mean time the day was waning, and the westering sun now hung low in the horizon. Waiting and watching we saw an overwhelming force of the enemy's cavalry sweeping over those plains, and driving our thin line, there stationed, before them in rapid retreat; thus leaving our left and left rear wholly unprotected; and notwithstanding the men on our line, in front and to our right, were successfully fighting east of Winchester on the same ground they held in the early morning, yet they were now necessarily compelled to retreat. And who can blame them? Or who can say, with the semblance of truth, that General Early and his little army were, in any way, blamable for a defeat by such overwhelming forces? And who, unless endowed with more temerity than truth can, or could, claim that any general and men could have done better, under like conditions? About sunset, General Ramseur's division, accompanied by a part of General Long's artillery and our brigade, also retreated from the field, fighting as they went, and halting, as rear-guard for the army, for the night, at Kernstown, three miles distant.

On the morning of the twenty-second our brigade, still dismounted, held the left center of General Lomax's division, which held the left of our battle-line at Fisher's Hill. In our front we had constructed a temporary breastwork out of the near-by timber. During the forenoon the enemy made intermittent attacks on our front and to our right which were repulsed. About 3 o'clock, General Crook was sent with a corps of infantry and a small force of cavalry to march beyond and around our left. The claim made, by such writers as those above mentioned, that this flank movement was not discovered until it was too late to meet it, is not correct. The fact was that General Lomax knew of the movement, but was, at the time, as was our whole line of battle, confronted by, and fighting with, vastly superior numbers of the enemy, and little, or no, force could be sent to meet Crook's corps. General Lomax did his best and tried to stop it with his almost unsupported artillery but failed. Five or six to one was too much odds. Our regiment did not start to retreat until we were enclosed in the vertex of an acute angle formed by the enemy's line in our front and that swinging around to our rear. Then we went and went fast and continued to go until, by our fleetness, we had distanced the foe. The boys said that the writer's speed-rate was well nigh miraculous. But again, as at Winchester, who, under the circumstances, that is intelligent and conscientious can blame us for running, or for the defeat that made it necessary?

CHAPTER XXXIV

WOODSTOCK AND VICINITY—
CEDAR CREEK—SHERIDAN'S RIDE

After passing Woodstock on our retreat from Fisher's Hill, our retirement, and General Sheridan's advance, [was] quite leisurely. Several skirmishes occurred on the way. General Early led his little army to Brown's Gap in the Blue Ridge. The Federal army followed us to Harrisonburg. Not withstanding his recent victories, General Sheridan had apparently concluded that the effort and cost spent in winning them had been so great that it would be better and safer to starve us out by burning our friends out, than to again try to out-fight us—better to wage war on non-combatants with fire, than to face our fire on a battle-line. A plan which, although somewhat cruel—perchance a little cowardly—was possibly good policy; at least he vigorously adopted it, and at once proceeded to complete the work of destruction already commenced by him and General Hunter. Collecting his army he retired to Cedar Creek; taking with him, or killing, nearly all the live stock, burning the barns and granaries, and most of the food, both for man and beast, not used by his army, as he went. Thereby leaving behind him many helpless families to face starvation during the coming winter. Uncivilized warfare, certainly, of which he later had the bad taste to boast. We pursued him. Our cavalry division advanced on the pike, and General Rosser's brigade on the back road to our left. On the 9th of October, I think, our company—then leading on the pike—had, from early dawn, been skirmishing with the enemy's rear guard. We had captured several of them—some in the act of burning and plundering—whom we, with difficulty, restrained our incensed men from killing.

As we neared Woodstock we saw that parts of it were burning. We charged, caught some of the men who had fired it, and stopped a few minutes to help extinguish the fires. We then rode on and were, soon again, skirmishing with our foes. Their resistance now became so stubborn that we were compelled to halt and await the coming of our comrades. While doing so, we noticed a few of the enemy in the fields to our left who were evidently trying to reach the pike in [the] rear of their own men, and some of us went after them. As we closed up they crossed a rough ravine and while following them, my horse in some way caught his foot and jerked his shoe, and with it a part of his hoof, entirely off. He nearly fell and I dismounted. We could now tell by the firing on our left that Rosser was rapidly retreating. Just then the enemy in force advanced on our men on the pike and all my near-by comrades, none of whom had crossed the drain, hastened at once to join in the resulting fight. It lasted several minutes before our men retreated—slowly at first, then more rapidly. I got my horse back across the drain too late to join them on the pike, so continued to retreat parallel to it through the fields. In the mean time, the forces battling on the pike had all passed on and left me in the rear.

So far I had not been noticed by the enemy; but now three of them saw me and came towards me. It was a critical situation, much more pleasant to contemplate now than then. Escape by flight was impossible. Many of their comrades were near, and as they came on I mounted but could only urge my crippled horse into a reluctant lope. They must have emptied their fire-arms in their late encounter, for they now dashed up with drawn sabers, ordered me to surrender, and took positions before, and to the right and left of me. The demand made for my surrender was refused. While dismounted I had loaded all the chambers of one of my pistols and now carried it in my hand. Therefore, even if they had empty pistols, their nearness made it dangerous for them to try to re-load them, and so we rode on, while they swore at and threatened me with instant death under their saber strokes, occasionally making demonstrations indicating an intention to carry out their threat. But, deterred, either by my already cocked pistol, or by the apparent certainty of my capture by themselves or comrades, they vented their wrath by continuing to swear at me. About this time the fight ahead had become more general and one of their regiments left the pike and formed in battle-line some two hundred and fifty yards before us. We were in rear of it and remained unseen; and I shaped our course toward its extreme right. We had nearly reached it, and I was about to make the rush around it for which I had been saving my horse and pistol, when a yell from its front—the sweetest music I had ever heard—proclaimed a charge by our men, and a moment later Lieutenant Jake Ward, backed by his company and regiment, appeared and I joined him among the scattering foe. In doing so I used my pistol, but not on any of the three Yankees mentioned. The enemy now retired. Later when I rejoined my company, I was, for the second time during the Valley campaign, compelled by my presence, to refute a report that I had been killed or captured—two fates that my comrades claimed I was, sometimes, over-anxious to shun.

This was wholly a cavalry fight between General Early's half-starved and equipped few and General Sheridan's over-fed and well-equipped many.

Finding that my horse was so badly crippled that he could not be used for some time, I left him where he would be well treated, obtained another, and saw him no more.

General Early moved on to Fisher's Hill, and we camped a few days in the Luray Valley. Our company knew but little about the actual fighting at the battle of Cedar Creek, fought on October 19th, 1864. We were much better acquainted with its cause and effect. For several days before this battle we encamped with our division in the Luray Valley, and, while scouting in the vicinity of Front Royal, I learned that a large part of General

Sheridan's army was already passing there on its way to join General Grant. That fact, as we then knew, was at once reported to General Early, then near Fisher's Hill. His orders were, and had been, to detain as far as possible these troops in the Valley. We are sure now, and so understood it then, that it was these orders and our report, possibly backed by his own natural inclination to fight, that induced him to advance upon and attack an entrenched enemy numbering three to his one.

So much for the cause, now for the effect. These departing troops were at once recalled and took part in the battle; and General Early was finally repulsed and retreated. But, in confirmation of what we, as soldiers and scouts, learned at the time, all reliable authority on the subject clearly indicates that General Sheridan was so badly crippled by this battle—in which his loss, except in artillery, was nearly double ours—that, although he retained all of his men apparently for the purpose, yet he made no further effort to drive General Early out of the Valley until long after the latter had sent nearly all of his little army to General Lee at Petersburg, nor until after 1864. If there was any other intelligent reason for General Sheridan's inactivity—What? Therefore the effect of this battle effectually accomplished its object. A few days after it occurred, General Sheridan sent a part of his cavalry force under General Powell up the Luray Valley as far as Milford, where it was defeated and driven back by our command, under General Lomax. Except for some unimportant skirmishes and scout fights, in most of which we took part, this ended the military operations in the Valley for the year 1864. Early went into camp at New Market, and Sheridan at Kernstown.

As above said, we took but little part in this Cedar Creek battle, but leaving part of our command at Front Royal to guard General Early's right flank, we arrived in rear of, and near to, the Federal army as it fell back from Cedar Creek, after the fighting in the early morning had ceased; and took position from some parts of which our pickets could see a long line of the enemy reforming just north of Middletown and could also see Newtown and the pike at several places between the two towns. Here we remained until late in the afternoon.

Various reasons have been given for Early's defeat at Cedar Creek. He said the main reason was because his few cavalry could not cope with the large cavalry force of the enemy, which remained intact, and was about as numerous as his whole army. General Kershaw was of the same opinion. We think they were correct, for we saw this mass of cavalry drawn up between us and the right wing of our advancing army. He further says that he was, to some extent, handicapped by the loss of some of his men who stopped in the enemy's camp to get something to eat. General Long says that if ever men were excusable for such alleged conduct, these half-starved men were. Experience inclines us to agree with Long. Early further says that, later in the day, some of his men retreated because seized with a panic. We think he was mistaken. Soldiers "who fight and run away" seldom, if ever, do so because panic-stricken. Panic can only result from a groundless fear, or one inspired by a trifling cause—a misapprehension of danger. It was not so here. And if soldiers never run unless seized with a panic, then many of the writer's comrades, who were accounted exceptionally brave, were, on several occasions, so seized, for they not only ran but they did so fast and long, and he was always among the foremost. "Eben Holden" said when enumerating his virtues, on his death bed, that he, "Never swore 'less 'twas nec' sary," and the writer feels sure that Confederate soldiers never ran until to do so was both a necessity and a virtue.*

The gallant General Gordon says that this final defeat was the result of an untimely halt for which General Early was responsible. The equally gallant General Kershaw, who in the early morning first broke through the Federal lines, does not seem to sustain him. The conclusion of the whole matter, as we understand it

---

* <u>Eben Holden</u> was a 1900 novel by Irving Bacheller

is: that 12,000 brave, intelligent men can not, and never could, successfully fight 36,000 men equally brave and intelligent. Hence the real reason for this defeat.

Now as to General Sheridan's celebrated ride. History leaves no room to doubt that he actually rode from Winchester to Middletown on the morning of October 19th, 1864, and that he arrived at the latter place about eleven o'clock on that day. It is equally well established by authentic history that before his arrival General Wright, his second in command, had rallied his troops and restored the battle near Middletown. Among other historical writers, both the Federal generals, Boynton and Carman, so state. The writer knows from personal observation, such to be the fact, but he does not know what general did the rallying. He also knows that he and some of his comrades remained in sight of the pike, over which the General rode, from eight o'clock in the morning until afternoon, and yet saw no stream of stragglers returning to the army at Middletown, as later claimed. Therefore all the glamour, glory and renown with which Read's poetical effusion emblazons this ride, are just about as fictitious and mythical as the existence of, and the many glorious attributes given to Barbara Frietchie, as portrayed by Whittier's poem. [See Appendix C for Read's poem "Sheridan's Ride"]

CHAPTER XXXV

***GENERAL EARLY'S VALLEY CAMPAIGN OF 1864—
AN UNEXPECTED FURLOUGH—THE ROUND BARN
INCIDENT—AN UNPLEASANT RIDE—AN ESCAPED
AMBUSH—IN THE VICINITY OF HUTTONSVILLE***

That General Early, about June 10th, 1864, was sent to the Valley with a detachment of about 9,000 men from General Lee's Richmond army; that the primary object of the expedition was for Early to meet and drive back General Hunter, who was approaching Lynchburg with about double his force; then to take such other action as, in his opinion, would best tend to create a diversion in General Lee's favor at Richmond where General Grant was pressing him with an overwhelming force; and that from the start Early was only leading a forlorn hope, are not only matters of truthful history, but are sustained by all attending facts. It is equally true that Early never had an effective force of more than 13,000 men in any of his Valley battles—never over 10,000 prior to the battle of Winchester—yet he was never theretofore defeated. General Long says that this campaign was remarkable, "For having accomplished more in proportion to the force employed, and for having given less public satisfaction than any other campaign of the war." Why? The General's answer is, "The want of appreciation of it is entirely due to the erroneous opinion that the city of Washington should have been taken, but this may be passed over as one of the absurdities of public criticism on the conduct of the war." Then why this lack of appreciation and erroneous opinion? Again the General's answer is that, "The boldness of Early's movements caused his force to be greatly exaggerated and rumor soon magnified it to four or five times its strength." He might have said "boldness and success."

General Early says in effect, that he preferred to suffer adverse criticism, rather than to injure the cause of the South by publishing the smallness of his numbers. Thus uninformed or unthinking writers, both in the North and South, who were not present, wrongfully criticised an able general and true patriot; forgetful or ignorant of the fact that he was with his 12,000 men carrying out his instructions by contending with 40,000 of the enemy, who, else, would have been assisting Grant to destroy Lee. The thoughtful student of truthful history will, perhaps, be surprised to learn, that the preponderance of force against which Stonewall fought at Kernstown—his only defeat—was no greater than that against which Early fought at Winchester, Fisher's Hill and Cedar Creek; and that in the three last named battles, except in artillery, the aggregate of the Federal loss exceeded ours. Why Sheridan, who was accounted a great general, and who here certainly led as brave men as ever fought for any cause, did not, with his overwhelming force sooner drive Early from the Valley, remains an open question. General Early can safely rest his fame on the opinion of General Lee, who wrote him on March 30th, 1865—eleven days before the latter surrendered—that his own confidence in the former's ability, zeal, energy, devotion and patriotism, remained unimpaired.

I have here made brief mention of General Early's campaign because I want my children to know the truth, as I understood it.

It is claimed that during this campaign, General Early fought some seventy-five battles and skirmishes worthy of note. Part of our company was engaged in most of them. From the 10th of June until about the 10th of November, the writer was on duty, of some kind, over half of the time. Returning from a scouting expedition to camp at Milford early one morning, about the date last mentioned, I met Doctor Bland. I had not seen him since early in September when he furnished me an ambulance in which to ride. He now went by me without speaking. I did not know why and soon turned to look after him. He was following me. He came up, shook hands, said he did not, at first, recognize me, looked me over and asked what was the matter. I told him nothing. He said he knew better, that I was completely run down from over-work, that if I did not stop it I would certainly die, and good-naturedly growling, left me; but on the same day handed me, unasked, a sixty-day furlough. Prior to this meeting with him, I had felt very tired, but nothing more. What he told me must have had some truth in it, else it scared me, or awoke my imagination so that I believed it to be true, for I now felt quite weak and found that I had lost some thirty pounds in weight. So I accepted the furlough and started homeward. After the close of the war, Doctor Bland claimed that this was the second, probably the third, time he had saved my life over my protest. The other times were when I was wounded at Chantilly and Smithfield.

Riding slowly and recuperating rapidly, I reached Mr. Samuel Sutton's home near Green Bank in Pocahontas County about a week after leaving the Valley. Mr. Sutton and his wife welcomed me, as always, with a kindness that was well-nigh parental. Here I found Lee Ward of Captain Marshall's company and Gene Isner of ours. Both wanted to go home; and after I had rested a day or two, we left our horses with Mr. Sutton and started on our way. Traveling warily, we reached the pike at Slaven's Cabin one evening just after dark, and walked over Cheat Mountain to the vicinity of Huttonsville—Lee's home—in the night. Extreme caution was necessary. Here we remained a few days, then proceeded by obscure paths to Gene's home on Isner's Run, spent a short time there and then moved on to my own home. Suffice it to say that we were enjoying ourselves immensely.

We now started on our return, traveling the by-paths until arriving in sight of the pike about two miles south of where Elkins now stands. It was now nearly night. From here we saw an ambulance, accompanied by two out-riders dressed in blue, driving by, going in the direction from which we came. We did not want the men, but the horses looked very desirable. Surmising that they would stop for the night at the hostelry of Mr. Ward, the owner of the Round Barn, we turned and followed them. Our inference proved correct. We found the soldiers—seven, in number—in the Ward house, and the four horses in the barn. The writer stood guard on the pike between the buildings, while his comrades led the horses out of the back door of the barn and a short distance southward through the field. It was now about 10 o'clock. Here we mounted and our ride began. We soon left the pike and in just twenty-four hours from the time we started, reached a friend's house a few miles north of Green Bank. We had a splendid lot of horses. The one that had belonged to Colonel Youart—then in command at Beverly—became mine. So far as we ever learned, our trail was never discovered. Certain it is that we were not followed.

Next morning Gene and Lee rode on to Mr. Sutton's, while I, taking the extra horse, which bore the U. S. brand, with me, went to a Mr. Taylor's who resided near Green Bank, and traded it for one not branded. That afternoon, leading the new horse, I started back to Randolph. Traveling most of the way by a rough trail through the woods, I timed myself so as to reach the pike where it crosses the left-hand branch of the Greenbrier River just at dark. The night was gloomy, there was no moon, and heavy clouds obscured the stars. The silence was oppressive. The road lonely, enclosed with foreboding forests, and with no inhabited homes on the way. To make it worse, I had been warned that the Federal scout, Slayton, with his squad, was somewhere on the road toward Beverly. I do not think I was superstitious or over-timid in reference to the supernatural—perhaps I was scared. Certainly the contemplation of that ride was, for some reason, not altogether pleasant. But I fastened the horse I was leading to the near side of mine, carried my pistol in my right hand, and made it at a moderate gait. Probably no one will ever know how awfully loud the impact of those horses' feet as they hit the ground seemed to me; or how many leagues I thought the sound we made, as we crossed the Cheat River bridge, could be heard. I had been in a few tight places during the war but, of all, this ride was about the most nerve-trying. Daylight found me at Alf Hutton's near Huttonsville. "Uncle Billy" Price was there. At my request he rode the horse, for which I had traded, to Mr. Mat Ward's, near Elkins. Ward, who was a friend of my father's, was buying horses for the Federal Government. I had instructed Mr. Price to tell Mr. Ward just how I had come by the horse, and to ask him for me, to take it to, and buy it from father. And it so turned out that on the fourth day after we left the Round Barn, my father got one hundred dollars in gold, for the horse for which I had traded the branded U. S. one.

Still riding my Colonel Youart horse—a regular daisy—I spent a few days very pleasantly at Huttonsville, and then returned to Green Bank. In the mean time Mr. Price returned and informed me of the result of his trip.

Upon returning to Green Bank, after my lonely night ride, about the middle of December, my intention had been to rejoin our command at once; but I now learned, from some of our men, who were stopping with Mr. Sutton, that it had been temporarily disbanded for the purpose of procuring food and forage during the winter. Very little of our cavalry force, except General Rosser's small brigade, had been retained in a cohesive body, west of the Blue Ridge. I now spent several days in looking up our scattered company; finding part of it in three different counties—Bath, Highland and Pocahontas. It had taken but little part in the fighting during my absence. A few of us now visited, and spent the holidays at and near Huttonsville. We had a pleasant time, but caution was necessary. It was while on this trip that John Phares and Walt Allen's men planned to ambush and kill me without giving me even a warning halt. The ambush was set on the path leading up on the east side of the river above the Scott ford, near the mouth of Mill Creek. The reason given the men for so acting, as some of them later informed my

Huttonsville friends, was that if halted I would either make my escape or kill some of them, possibly do both. Fortunately I passed the position selected a few minutes before my enemies arrived there. Later, after I had learned the facts, opportunity was given me to retaliate on Phares, and I thought of this circumstance, but let him pass on in safety. Early in January we again went South and scattered. I proceeded to Highland County and stopped with the family of Mr. Absalom Crawford—refugees from our county, who were living on Jackson's River. While there I learned of General Rosser's move on Beverly and started rapidly after him; picking up Ad Currence of Captain Marshall's Company, on the way. We were too late, and only in time to meet that part of his command which recrossed Cheat Mountain from Huttonsville near its western top. Currence and I then separated. He went to Elk Water, and I on to Huttonsville. I had no adventure; but Ad met, charged upon, and had his horse killed by two deserters who escaped. Ad was not hurt. He procured another horse, later rejoined me, and together we rode on toward Beverly, where we had learned the enemy were again reassembling after the retirement of General Rosser.

When we arrived at the point of a hill from whence we had a plain view of the town, we discovered that an unmistakable commotion, accompanied by a noise as of moving wagons, was going on therein and beyond. We also saw a few blue-coated horsemen drawn up in the street, but rode on and stopped near Files' Creek in the southern end of the town. In a few minutes we turned back and, without trouble, and, so far as we knew, without being followed rode slowly back to Huttonsville.

Just about this time, the enemy evacuated Beverly, but established posts at Philippi and Buckhannon, from which on alternate days they scouted to, and occasionally beyond, that point.

After spending some time pleasantly and undisturbed at Huttonsville, the writer returned to Green Bank. Here we organized a squad of about fifteen Randolph County soldiers, mostly from the companies of

Marshall and Hutton, with the intention of returning to and making a more extended stay at Huttonsville.

Our squad of some fifteen Randolph County men, arrived in the vicinity of Huttonsville early in February and remained there until late in March. Lieutenant J. G. Ward and the writer were the only officers among them. Later Colonel Hutton spent a few days there with us. Notwithstanding the gloom that then overshadowed our cause, our boys, together with their lady friends—many of whom were as beautiful as the Houris—contentedly enjoyed themselves. It was well. They held numerous dances at many private homes. We will not undertake to describe any of these, individually or in detail. Suffice it to say that these young people considered them eminently successful. The writer, who had never learned the art of tripping "the light fantastic toe,"* took no actual part in these dances; but unless held at some isolated homestead, [he] could always be found on the road between the dancers and their enemies, where occasionally he proved of use and his friends were not disturbed.

THE WOUNDED CAPTAIN HILL

Captain Ben Hill who had, when he made his raid on Beverly, on October 29th, 1864, been severely wounded and left there, still remained at the home of Mr. Adam Crawford. About the middle of February, we concluded that if able to travel, we would take him South, and with some eight or ten of our best mounted men, rode to Beverly for that purpose. We found the Captain in a pitiable condition, very weak, but willing and anxious to try to make the trip to Dixie. In the mean time a squad of Federal cavalry—about equal to us in number—had come over from Buckhannon and were now watching us from the hill at the forks of the road west of the bridge. They made no attempt to come nearer the town while we remained there. No shooting occurred. A lieutenant,

---

* Milton, "*L'Allegro*" (1632) l.34

named Howertsey[*] I think, had also been wounded in this raid, left at Mr. Lemuel Chenoweth's and was still there; but, as we were informed, was too weak to be moved. Before starting I called to see him, found him alone in his bed room and told him we were going to remove Captain Hill and asked if he were able to go with us. Groaningly but emphatically, he answered that he was not. From his actions and talk I concluded that his death was imminent and turned to leave. Just then one of Mr. Chenoweth's daughters, who knew me by sight, came in and addressed me by name and rank. In response to an exclamation I turned to find the Lieutenant sitting up in bed and looking at me with his soul in his eyes. He quickly asked Miss Chenoweth to repeat my name and she did so. He had apparently heard it before, for he jumped out of bed, struck the floor, waltzed a few steps, let go several naughty expletives, and boastingly informed us that physically he was about as good as new. It was true. He had for some time been playing "possum" because he feared the Yankees (one of whom he had taken me to be) would, as he expressed it, tote him to some Northern prison. Unaided he walked to, and took a seat in, our wagon, and placing the Captain on a pallet therein, we drove carefully away and reached Huttonsville that evening. Here, at the home of Colonel Hutton, both our wounded comrades had a good night's rest, and next morning we sent them on their way, rejoicing. Both entirely recovered.

---

[*] In his Feb 8, 1865 report, Capt. C. H. Evans, 8th Ohio Volunteer Cavalry, says Capt. Harding took Capt. Hill and Lt. Towerson away.

CHAPTER XXXVI

RETURN TO OUR COMMAND—
SUSPENSE [ABOUT LEE'S SURRENDER]—
WE MEET CAPTAIN BADGER'S FEDERAL SQUADRON—
I FIRE MY LAST WAR SHOT

We left Huttonsville and joined our reassembling brigade in Rockbridge County late in March, 1865, and crossed the Blue Ridge on our way, as we then supposed, to join General Lee's army at Petersburg; but a few days later, returned, recrossed the Ridge and encamped near Covington. In the mean time Colonel Arnett had taken such a fancy to my Yankee horse, that a trade between us, in which my horse was valued at $3000 and his at $1000, resulted. For the difference he gave me his note for $1400 and a watch valued at $600. Therefore, I once owned and rode a $3000 horse, and later carried a $600 watch.

By now all thinking men must have recognized the imminency of the certain overthrow of the Confederacy. Certainly many of the soldiers did and, as a result, some of the less determined were slow to respond to this last call to arms. Among others, a few of the Randolph and the Pocahontas County men, who had wintered at home, while disbanded to forage for food, and who had not been notified of the call, failed to meet us; and Lieutenant Ward and I were sent back after them. We reached the vicinity of Huttonsville on the 5th of April. The enemy, commanded by a Colonel Hall I think, now occupied Beverly in considerable force, and we had to be cautious; but looked up and made arrangements with the boys we found there to get ready and meet us on Becca's Creek on the tenth prepared to start South. While waiting for them to

187

assemble, Lieutenant Ward, one of his men and I, on foot, visited my home near where Read Station is now located. We started to return on the ninth, and that evening intercepted the U. S. Mail on its way to Beverly, on the pike, a short distance south of the present site of Elkins. The contents of the mail-bags pretty clearly indicated that a few of the Beverly girls were corresponding with Yankee soldiers. They also included a telegram to the Federal commander there, stating that General Lee had surrendered his army that morning. We did not believe the telegram, nor approve of the correspondence; so, over our own signature, and in unmistakable diction we endorsed our disbelief on the telegram and our disapproval on the letters; and sent them on by the carrier just at night-fall. We later learned from one who happened to be present when the Beverly commandant received and read this telegram, that the latter's remarks anent our endorsement thereon were about equally punctuated with laughter and profanity.

We now moved on by a path which traversed the hills through the Wees settlement, east of Beverly, and were ascending a low ridge when a squad of men, who proved to be Yankees, appeared on its top about twenty-five yards ahead. Our relative positions favored us. They were above with a background of skylight; while we were below in the shadows of the surrounding hills; but they had at least four men to our one. Mutual halts were given and inquiries as to who we were [were] made. As a corruption of the word, boss, our boys had nicknamed me, Bosier; and now speaking for my companions and self, I replied to their inquiry and repeated ours by saying, "I am Bosier, sir, who are you?" Divested of much unorthodox language, the answer, "We'll bosier you," accompanied by a high-flying shower of lead, was thrown back viciously toward us; and thus our bloodless skirmish opened. Doubtless, "distance lent enchantment,"* to the beautiful music made by their singing bullets as they cut through

---

* Thomas Campbell, "Pleasures of Hope" Part 1, 1. 7

the night-air above us. However, the situation called for immediate action—and we acted. My gun snapped, but those of my companions answered at once; and now relying on the lights and shadows around us; the stentorian voice of Lieutenant Jake, which had never yet failed us in volume or effect; the known gallantry of my comrades, and our already drawn revolvers; I directed a yell and a charge. Both were delivered with prompt, vigorous and forceful effectiveness; and thus the fiasco closed. When we reached the abandoned hilltop, our enemies, some of whom had been mounted, still favored us with the pleasant music made by their rapid retreat through the adjoining forest.

We now moved forward on the opened path toward Becca's Creek and arrived there about noon next day; and at once started South with our assembled men as planned; but on account of rain and high water did not reach Dunmore, where we had another squad awaiting us, until the evening of the thirteenth. As we moved on next morning we found the country rife with unconfirmed reports of General Lee's surrender.

Filled with suspense, anxiety and apprehension which bordered on despair, we arrived late in the night of the sixteenth at Sweet Sulphur Springs. Here we received positive confirmation of General Lee's surrender, and of the disbandment of our brigade, pending the result. The tidings were fraught with bitterness to us, but we were powerless to right the wrong we felt. Most of our men now sought their scattering brigade comrades. A few of us turned back homeward to await developments. On the 18th of April (Not of May as erroneously given in Maxwell's Randolph County History), eleven of us, under no particular leader, met Captain Badger's squadron, on the Warm Springs Pike—about where Minnehaha Park is now located, I think. We came from the east. Ad Ward and the writer were riding in front when we ran into the enemy's advance. As prearranged we all charged at once, drove them back and captured one of them; but coming in sight of their main force, left the pike and rode on obliquely thereto through an old field, to the point of the ridge where we halted, and from whence, at a distance of some three hundred yards, we had an unobstructed view of all our foes. They were soon charging past us on the pike, where we had left one man with our prisoner, and up the hill toward us; preceded by an ineffectual shower of pistol balls. When we first halted, we discovered one of them, who had escaped from their advance when we charged it, circling the ridge in our front. He was on foot and bareheaded, but refused to stop when first ordered. However, our second pistol ball brought him to time. He threw up his hands, came up to us and proved to be our old enemy, Sheriff Phares. Our greeting was short. There was but little time for an exchange of compliments. He intimated that we were included in Lee's surrender. We did not agree. Later he claimed that I threatened to kill him if he repeated his remarks. Of course he was mistaken. The Yankees were now almost upon us. We had no inclination or ability to take Phares with us; so we impolitely turned our backs upon him, and ran so rapidly that we overtook the head of our little squad on a bench of the ridge a short distance from where we left him. I was again splendidly mounted, but several of my comrades were riding less speedy horses; and, in order to save them from capture by the fast approaching enemy, Lieutenant Ward, his brother Ad and I dismounted, gave our horses to our men to lead, started them on, and stepped back to the brow of the hill-bench to try to check the on-coming foe. It was time. My pistols were empty, and those of my companions nearly so; but I had my Spencer. The head of their charging column was now within fifty yards of us; and through the intervening shrubbery we gave them a couple of volleys, which caused considerable confusion among, but did not altogether stop, them. As planned my two comrades now left the path, while I with my Spencer still ready and presented, stood my ground a few moments longer. A man riding a fleet dun horse led their advance. On account of the foliage near the path-side, he, apparently, did not see me until less than thirty yards distant. He then made an effort to check his horse which raised its head simultaneously with the flash of my gun. The bullet sped true, found lodgment in its brain, and horse and rider went over backward among the latter's immediate followers. The resultant check gave us time to get away from the path and out of sight before they reached our position, and they passed us by and hurried on. We examined the fallen horse and equipment, but found nothing of value that we could carry away, except the bridle. We remained near until the enemy returned, on both sides of us, to the pike—taking their comrade's saddle with them; then [we] went on and stopped for the night, at Mr. Cleek's on Knapp's Creek. Next morning some of our scattered squad joined us there, and informed me that my horse had been needlessly lost. Regrets for their carelessness availed me nothing; and I had other horses.

We now determined to part to meet at Mr. Sutton's near Green Bank on the twenty-seventh, from whence we would attempt to join General Johnston's command. A remote day was set so as to give all who wished to go with us time to get ready and assemble. With this arrangement made, Lieutenant Ward and I, on foot and alone, started for Huttonsville, and so traveling reached there on the twentieth, very tired, but still hopefully determined. That night the returning Captain Badger camped near the home of Lieutenant Ward, while the writer slept, as the just sleep, at Colonel Hutton's nearby. Next day the Captain moved on to Beverly. I rested. Lieutenant Ward returned at once to Pocahontas County.

Captain Badger made a report of this affair which will be found on pages 1312 to 1314, Volume 95 of the Official Records of the "War Of The Rebellion"; from which the following are extracts:

"My advance was suddenly and furiously attacked. I immediately threw my three companies into shape to make a strong fight if the enemy were in force, and to pursue instantly if he were not. I galloped forward to see what it was. I found that the enemy were running up the side of the mountain to get away; told Lieut. McConkey to take his company instantly up the hill after them and shove them at top speed; told sergeant Llewellyn to dash ahead after a few who had ran back on the road by which they came. He captured one who said it was a squad of 25, with Major (Elihu) Hutton, Captain (J. W.) Marshall, and Captain (J. F.) Harding, going to their homes. I expected to find that Captain Harding and friends had gathered a pretty good squad through the mountains to bushwhack us on Greenbrier or about the Gum road on Cheat Mountain. Therefore I placed half my Spencers in the advance guard and half in the rear. Moved on, reached White's, top of Cheat Mountain. An hour before sundown stopped for supper. Learned that Captain Harding had passed there in the middle of the day with five men, armed and on foot, saying he was going to Beverly. He also said that my command was returning on that road and would reach White's some time that evening. I studied a good deal as to his intentions. His character is such that I felt sure he was not going to surrender. Finally I concluded that he had gathered up thirty or forty men, and had them coming through the mountains by Becca's Creek, and either intended to entangle us in a blockade in going down the mountain, and cut us up, or to surprise us after we encamped in the valley. It is eight miles from White's to Stipe's (foot of mountain). I had Sergeant Knott with ten men and an ax march half a mile ahead and look for a blockade; commenced the descent at nine p. m. Reached Stipe's without accident, and learned that Harding with one man had passed there just at dark, saying he was going to Beverly to give himself up. This left four of his men unaccounted for, which made me look still more for another party acting with him. I had twenty men dismounted, go ahead, and in two squads search every house within three miles of Huttonsville for Harding and Ward (whose mother lives close by), but found no trace whatever of them. Moved into the valley and bivouacked near Mrs. Ward's, making as much noise as possible to let the enemy know I was there, it being my wish that he attempt a surprise. Next day moved on to Beverly, arriving at 5 p. m. As Captain Harding has not made his appearance nor been heard of at a late hour to-night, I have no doubt he had some designs against us. He had no chance."

The gallant Captain's presentation of this affair, as appears from the above extracts from his report makes "Much Ado About Nothing."*

A resume of the actual facts shows: That Colonel Hutton was not with us and that there were only eleven men in our squad when we first met and so furiously attacked the enemy; that only two of us, with no support, crossed Cheat Mountain ahead of them; that it was utterly impossible for us to know when, or upon what road they would return; and that on the night they searched every house within three miles of Huttonsville and encamped in the valley with much braying, the writer slept unsearched for and undisturbed by noise, at the home of Colonel Hutton, less than one mile from either their bivouac or Huttonsville. Therefore, and beyond all question, the Captain's cogitations and conclusions were wholly without foundation; ridiculously absurd, and could only have been prompted by undue timidity or excessive buncombe; and his action, as he gives it, must have resulted from unnecessary caution that barely—if at all—missed the border line of cowardice.

---

* Title of a Shakespeare comedy, ca. 1600.

CHAPTER XXXVII

A FEW DAYS IN RANDOLPH—RETURN TO GREEN BANK FAILURE—GENERAL LEE

I remained at Huttonsville, alone, until the morning of the twenty-third, when "Dixie John" Pritt joined me. We spent the following two days in visiting his home, which was then a short distance north of the present site of Valley Bend. Here we were kindly welcomed and splendidly entertained by his family and people. While there we intended, should opportunity offer, to try to capture a couple of Yankee horses, upon which to ride back to Dixie; but we found no cavalry south of Beverly. We then started on our return to Green Bank, and reached Mr. Sutton's near there on the evening of the twenty-seventh as planned.

Upon arriving at Mr. Sutton's we were met by unconfirmed rumors of General Johnston's surrender, and the boys who were still in that vicinity thought it best to remain there pending further information. Before the coming of these rumors, some of them had moved on toward the Warm Springs. Mounting one of my horses, which had been kept by Mr. Sutton since we had left Huttonsville in March, alone I started after them and reached the top of Warm Springs Mountain on the twenty-ninth, where I found them halted by more definite news of Johnston's surrender which still lacked confirmation. However, we received word from General Rosser that he would, with his command, meet us all in Staunton on the 10th of May, ready to lead us to any organized Confederate force still fighting in the South. Deferred hope is less bitter than despair. Most of our comrades now determined to, and did, surrender. A few of us concluded to meet General Rosser, as suggested.

Again we separated. Alone, the writer returned to Huttonsville on the 2nd of May and remained there and near there until the fifth. Late that evening, learning that a detachment of Federal cavalry had just gone over Cheat Mountain on its way to Pocahontas County, I immediately followed after them, and reached Mr. Sutton's on the next day. The enemy had passed on toward Pendleton County. None of our boys, except Squire Kittle, met me at Mr. Sutton's. So far as I then knew, or now know, all the others had already surrendered. Squire and I now started on our way to meet General Rosser at Staunton on the date formerly set; and arrived at Mr. Cross's in Augusta County on the ninth. Here we learned that a Federal force, to which General Rosser and all his command had also surrendered, then occupied Staunton. Next morning we moved back toward McDowell, but Squire soon turned, went on to Staunton and surrendered. Alone and troubled but hopeful that our trans-Mississippi army was still in the field, I started thitherward and stayed at Mr. McLaughlin's on Jackson's River, below the Warm Springs, on the night of the thirteenth. Next morning, just while preparing to move on by way of Lewisburg, I learned, from what appeared to be a reliable source, that the western army, or the greater part of it, had also surrendered. History informs us that the last skirmish of the war occurred at Brazos Santiago, Texas on that day—May 13th, 1865.

Again slowly, and indescribably lonely, I turned toward Randolph and—home! And, "All that poets sing, and grief hath known, of hopes laid waste, knells in that word—Alone!"

With the coming of the year, 1865, also came, under the policy then and thereafter pursued by President Davis and his Cabinet, the beginning of the end of the life of the Confederacy, and, therefore, of the War. Although unacknowledged, even to themselves, all well informed, intelligent, thinking citizens of the South, must have—at least should have—recognized that fact. Certainly all her front-line soldiers did. How could it have been otherwise? On all those lines, her half-starved, half-clothed, quarter-shod and badly equipped defenders were facing overwhelming numbers of her well-fed, well-clothed, well-shod and splendidly equipped foes. Her resources, both in men and means, were exhausted. She could not succor her fast waning armies from either. Her heroic women and helpless children—our loved ones at home—were actually suffering for want of the food necessary to sustain life. General Lee's glorious little Army was the only bulwark upon which the South depended—all that stood between her capital and General Grant's multitudinous host—and if Lee's army were lost, all would be lost, as the sequel proved. Moved by these adverse conditions, General Lee made frequent calls upon his government for men and maintenance for them. He received no adequate response. He informed the Confederate authorities of the dire result to be expected, unless supported as requested. Still they did not, could not, comply. He then advised, and even initiated, a retreat while it was possible to do so, but they rejected his advice and stopped his movement. Why President Davis and his Cabinet should expect General Lee, with his suffering army to hold in check General Grant's thrice-superior army in men, and ten time superior in equipment and sustenance, is passing strange. But why they should require him to do so until the meshes thrown around him made it impossible for him to extricate his famished army, is wholly incomprehensible; yet so they did. But our high-souled General Lee, to whom the world then paid homage—as it yet pays it to his memory—went uncomplainingly on in the discharge of his duty, as set before him by his conscience, the rulers of his government and his fealty to his State. Yet, all the while, as shown by his conversations, writings and acts, the great and tender heart of Lee, the man, was shedding tears of blood, over the impending doom of a cherished principle which he approved as right; over the death-knell of the cause of the South, for which the lives of many of her best and bravest had been, and were still being, sacrificed; over the accumulating distress stalking everywhere within her borders; over the continued suffering of her soldiers—comrades all—and over the anguish and desolation which enshrouded all her people, whom he loved. This was his Gethsemane.

And we soldiers of lesser note, "To fortune and to fame unknown,"* following, in our pursuit of duty, the example set by our peerless leader, and catching the spirit of the old-time Christian martyrs, determined to suffer on; to fight on; to face danger and death; and, if need be, to sacrifice our lives on duty's altar, rather than to voluntarily abandon the defense of a cause—no matter how utterly hopeless such defense might be—which all our inherited patriotic traditions and teachings had taught us to believe was right. Yes! and which, to us, was right.

General Lee needs no eulogy from tongue or pen; but that pronounced by Professor Philip Stanley Worsley, and sent to him with a translated copy of Homer's story of the fall of Troy, is so beautifully appropriate that we here append it.

> The grand old bard that never dies,
> Receive him in our English tongue;
> I send thee, but with weeping eyes,
> The story that he sung.
>
> Thy Troy is fallen, thy dear land
> Is marred beneath the spoiler's heel;
> I cannot trust my trembling hand
> To write the things I feel.
>
> Ah, realms of tombs! but let her bear
> This blazon to the last of times;
> No nation rose so white and fair,
> Or fell so pure of crimes.
>
> The widow's moan, the orphan's wail
> Come round thee, yet in truth be strong;
> Eternal right, though all else fail,
> Can never be made wrong.

---

* Thomas Gray, "On a Distant Prospect of Eaton College" (Epitaph)

An angel's heart, an angel's mouth,
Not Homer's, could alone for me
Hymn well the great Confederate South,
Virginia first, and Lee!

CHAPTER XXXVIII

I WRITE MY OWN PAROLE AND SURRENDER— [ONE LAST DANGER]—HOME

> "Then black Despair,
> The shadow of a starless night, was thrown
> Over a world in which I moved alone."

The magnanimous General Lee said at Appomattox that he would rather die than surrender, and later expressed regret that he had not fallen in one of his last battles, and I suppose that we of humbler station and less responsibility, to some extent, felt the same; for while it is barely possible that, unrecognized, I still retained a lingering hope for the success of our cause, yet certain it is that as I now proceeded on my lonely way toward Huttonsville, along a road upon which my armed enemies might have been met at any moment, I did not then contemplate surrendering, no matter what the immediate issue might be. And so traveling I came to Huttonsville about the 17th of May, 1865; still undetermined as to my future course and for a few days remained in retirement while I communicated with my family. On the twenty-first I saw a copy of General Lee's farewell address to his soldiers. It was short but abounded in beautiful sentiment; tersely but eloquently expressed. I then copied and retained that part of it which referred to his parting with them and their return to their several homes in the following language—"You will take with you, the satisfaction that proceeds from a consciousness of duty faithfully performed; and I earnestly pray that a merciful God will extend to you His blessing and protection." The language of this address, coming from such a source, in connection with other information then received, left me no further room to hope for our cause, or to doubt that the war was over. "Do the duty which lies nearest you" was ever General Lee's motto.

On that same evening, Father came to me with a message from my mother and sisters. They had heard an unfounded report that I intended going to Mexico; but I well knew that, next to my duty to Virginia's cause, was that due from me to my parents and sisters. And since, according to General Lee's address, our duty to our cause had been not only faithfully performed but had ceased to exist, it needed not this appeal from my own loved ones to determine me to go to them, and I assured Father that I would do so in a very few days. He was satisfied; remained at Huttonsville that night, and before starting back, next morning, advised me not to travel on the pike, or pass through Beverly on my way home. I then, for the first time, learned that because I had been implicated in the wounding of Sheriff Phares on the Imboden raid, my friends expected trouble between him and his family and myself. This did not change my contemplated movements.

On the morning of May 23, 1865, I mounted my horse and rode to the home of Mr. Wash Ward. A little later I saw a company of Federal soldiers ride up to and dismount at, the residence of Mr. Abe Hutton's family, about three hundred yards distant. Then writing my own parole, to which I signed my own and Captain Marshall's names—the latter being authorized to issue them, I rode down to where the Yankees, several of whom were still standing in the door-yard, had halted. I was armed with three pistols, and our foes watched my approach with evident curiosity. Their commander, when inquired for, was summoned from the house and came out to where I was sitting on my horse. We passed mutual introductions. He laughed, shook hands and said he had guessed who I was, from what he had learned. He was Captain Beckel from Ohio [Lafayette Bechtel, Eighth Ohio Volunteer Cavalry]. I presented my parole. He smiled as he looked at it, but said that the war was over and it would answer its purpose. He invited me to dismount, go into the house where most of his men were, and take a seat; all of which I did. Sheriff Phares was sitting in the room, with a dark frown on his brow and no greeting on his tongue. Without apparently addressing any one in particular, he at once commenced to abuse the cause of the South and all concerned in upholding it. This was hard for me to take; and when, among other things, he said that my brother Marion, who had fallen in a skirmish at which he (Phares) was present deserved the fate he there met, I could not, at least I did not, [any] longer quietly do so.

I did not then know whether or not the Captain was listening to what was being said, or what would be his attitude if he were. Doubtless I thought it would be inviting my own certain death; but arising and drawing one of my pistols, I told Phares to do the same, as that would give him an equal chance for his life, but that I intended to kill him. He hesitated. I did not think want of courage made him do so. Indeed I was sure it did not; but apparently he relied upon interference by his comrades. The situation was tense, and, to us all, must have augured tragedy. I was facing Phares with my cocked pistol in my hand, and could almost feel the presence, and could certainly hear the labored breathing, of his comrades behind me, and had just repeated my demand that he arise, draw his pistol and so meet me on equal terms, because one of us must die, when Captain Beckel, who had in fact heard all that was said, stepped between us, pushed me back with his arm, and commenced cursing Phares; telling him, among other things, that he had saved his life but doubted that it was right to do so, because his (Phares') language was not only ungentlemanly but wholly unbearable.

Captain Beckel was one of nature's noblemen, and was leading men of like character, for when he told Phares that he had saved his life, and the latter claimed that these men should have shot me from the rear, they indignantly disclaimed all intention or inclination to do so. From what the Captain said, I am not sure that he intended to interfere if Phares had tried to defend himself. He did not seem to blame me, and only remarked that it would probably be safer, both for myself and the other fellows, if I were less handy with my pistols, which he admitted I was entitled to carry. Thus our first interview pleasantly ended. He invited me to call at his office in Beverly when convenient, and we parted with mutual good wishes, each for the other's future. That was just fifty-three years ago. During that interval I have met many other Federal soldiers, who gallantly faced and fought us in the war-time; and all such—even as did Captain Beckel and his men—have uniformly, and at all times, treated me well and kindly. A few, who did not so meet and fight us, did not, at the dawn of the peace-time, so pleasant and kindly meet us.

Traveling through the Phares community, I started for home on the 24th of May, 1865; a little over four years since first leaving there for the army. About a mile south of Beverly I met Thomas B. Scott, who told me that Benjamin Phares, Sheriff Phares' father, was already there for the purpose of getting a warrant issued for my arrest for complicity in the wounding of the latter on the Imboden raid; and he earnestly insisted that I either turn back or pass around Beverly. But while I thanked, I did not heed him and rode on. Before reaching the town, Mr. Scott, riding rapidly, overtook me. Asked why he turned back, he said that he had determined to be with and stand by me if trouble awaited me. It was a generous intention for which I then thanked him, and for which he always held a warm place in my friendship; but I preferred to, and did, face the situation alone.

Upon entering Captain Beckel's office, I found him and Mr. Phares, whom I only slightly knew, engaged in a violent altercation in reference to my arrest. Phares insisted that it be made at once; but the Captain refused to move in the matter; saying that, pursuant to the rules of civilized warfare, the wounding of his son was justifiable. Except for the greeting by name and rank which the Captain gave me when entering his office—thereby adding fuel to Phares' ire, they were both so angry that for some time they took no further notice of my presence. Somehow I did not feel like resenting what this old man said about me and mine, as I would have resented it coming from his son. He was old and gray; even as my own father was old and gray. Viewing the whole transaction with a father's eye, doubtless it appeared to him that his boy had been wrongfully wounded. Therefore, I could appreciate and to some extent excuse his hostility toward myself; and at some length and as kindly as I could I told him so; but at the same time and very distinctly I gave him to understand that no apology was due from me to any one in reference to the matter under consideration, or in fact to any one for any war-time act of mine. The old man left me considerably mollified; and I heard nothing more on the subject of my arrest. Later the Phares family, including the wounded ex-sheriff, all became quite friendly with me. Captain Beckel, who had been an interested listener to my conversation with Mr. Phares, now remarked that he was glad to know that I could, under some circumstances, use my tongue as readily and effectively as I could my pistols, under others. Thanking him for the compliment, I told him that having three pistols and but one tongue, I could better spare one of the former than the latter, and that if he would accept one of my pistols as a memento of my appreciation for the great kindness he had shown me, I should be pleased to make him a present of it. He said that he would gladly accept and highly prize it for the giver's sake; and so I gave him choice of the three. He was a gallant foe, whom I have neither seen nor heard from since we then shook hands and parted in amity.

I reached home that same evening, found all well and awaiting my coming. Father and Mother had both aged rapidly during the four years of the war. They had apparently bravely borne the loss of their two darling boys, but silent grief had left its indelible imprint on face and form; and while the rose-colored future still lay unopened before my youthful sisters, it was sadly mingled with the Cypress of the past. Ah! we may seek to hide our sorrows behind a smiling face, but every heart best knows its own bitterness.

The welcome given me, by all those whom I then best loved, was rendered still more pleasant by their apparent Lethe of the past, their joyousness over our present meeting, and their abiding hope for the future. For me the war was now over, absolutely; and gathering up the broken life-strands as best I could, I turned my back upon the buried past and faced and moved on toward the unknown future.

Afterword

One reason an editor chooses an Afterword over an Introduction is to keep the reader's focus on the primary text. Captain Joseph French Harding's remarkable story has easily identifiable elements: a protagonist and several antagonists; an adventurous journey from home and back; pathos (Harding's two brothers dying within a few months of each other); the humor of men under stress (indexed as "Battlefield humor"); and two dramatic layers (the larger one of the War itself and the additional drama of having one's home county occupied by enemy troops—for four years!). In short, it is a "good read."

But Harding's memoirs also offer valuable historical insights into (1) the effects of the war in western (West) Virginia; (2) being a member of Stonewall Jackson's "foot cavalry" in his Shenandoah Valley Campaign; (3) being a company commander; and (4) being a Confederate cavalry officer in the strangely fluid and desperate last year of the War.

If the reader has turned here before he or she has read the memoirs, I would suggest reading only Appendix B, which is part of a letter Harding wrote to Maggie Hutton sometime between the Fall of 1862 and Winter of 1863. Unlike the memoirs, which are written fifty-six years after the events described, the letter is contemporary with them. It shows an early version of Harding's intelligence, his writing skills, his passion for the cause, and his love of his home in Randolph County, West Virginia.[*]

---

[*] For clarity, and assuming that likely readers of this text know the western counties of Virginia became a state in 1863, I identify locations in this Afterword and in the Index as we know them today. Randolph County is still a beautiful and rural area—over 1000 square miles with a population of only 27,000 people. Almost 30% of it is in the Monongahela National Forest, and east coast skiers will know the nearby resorts of Snowshoe and Canaan Valley.

The gossipy tone of the last page of the letter reminds us that these combatants were very young (Harding was twenty-two when the War started) and that they were postponing what young men and women normally did at this time of their lives.

The letter also reminds us that Company F of the 31st Virginia Infantry (like most companies) was composed of brothers, cousins, neighbors, and schoolmates. Many men in Company F had been working at or attending the Huttonsville Academy, a co-educational learning institution in south central Randolph County, which existed from 1854 to May of 1861. The memoirs reveal that Harding's ties to his classmates from the Huttonsville Academy were particularly strong. And Harding's election as the commander of Company F on May 1, 1862 shows the respect of the men for him.

The primary reason to use an Afterword is to answer questions that might be raised by the text itself. Any personal memoir or autobiography raises two major questions: what else do we know about the writer? and how reliable is the narration? In one sense, Is the writer being truthful? While it almost seems insulting to question the integrity of Harding—who clearly prides himself on his high moral and ethical standards, today's readers have been conditioned to question those who present themselves as our leaders and potential heroes. Given that Harding describes himself as a "skeptic" at the end of Chapter XX, he would probably be sympathetic to our search for authenticity in today's world.

An old adage says, "Every man is the hero of his own story"—and Harding's memoirs are no exception to this rule. He was known all his life for bravery and narrow escapes during the war. These things are mentioned in the county histories and in his obituary. His contemporaries had many years to challenge these stories, but apparently they did not. In fact some of Harding's data do not coincide with what we *now* know to be facts, and many of his battle assessments clearly reflect his strong Confederate bias. However, there is no evidence to suggest he was not being truthful in this recounting of his memories. Harding, like many other veterans of this and every war, probably did polish and, perhaps, embellish some of the stories. He even jokes in the memoirs about how his veteran comrades teased him when they got together to recount their "glory days." But when your comrades are teasing you for your swiftness, endurance, and marksmanship, you are either very good or very bad. The fact these men elected him to be their leader—in war and peace— probably attests to the former.

To substantiate every incident in the memoirs would be an impossible task. For example, did the conversations between Harding and Major Harry Gilmor take place as Harding describes? Major Gilmor's own reminiscences, *Four Years in the Saddle* written in 1866, provide limited support. Gilmor was probably trying to protect some of the people he rode with, since in 1866 they were still looked upon by many as traitors. He frequently uses only the first initials of their last names when describing an incident. We can tell from the histories, such as the *19th and 20th Virginia Cavalry* by Richard L. Armstrong, that Harding and Gilmor were sometimes riding together in the last twelve months of the war. And Gilmor does mention the well known Confederate sympathizer known as "Aunt Mary" of Newtown (now Stephen's City), VA. As Harding explains in his narration, "Aunt Mary" was truly his aunt—his mother's sister—Mary Elliott Nisewanger. Gilmor calls her, "my old friend Aunt Mary" (*Four Years*, 262). So the probability that they had dinner together at her house—and did some of the other things Harding describes— seems very high.

One other incident deserves special mention: the action Harding describes in Chapter XIV, the Battle of Cedar Mountain. Both Robert K. Krick, in *Stonewall Jackson at Cedar Mountain*, and John M. Ashcraft, Jr., in *31st Virginia Infantry*, cite General Jubal Early's August 14, 1862 report of the incident in which Harding says he had a central role. Early says:

A body of men from the thirty-first Virginia Regiment, around their colors, advancing in the same way, attracted my attention by their gallantry. I was particularly struck by the bravery exhibited by the color bearers of these two regiments, who, with these small bodies of men around them, were waving their flags in the very front, as if to attract a fire upon them, and advancing all the while.

After describing the deaths of Israel Marks, John Lewis, and the severe wounding of Perry Lewis, Harding says on pages 60-61:

My immediate later action is to me now inexplicable. Probably I then had no reason for it, other than the knowledge that some of my comrades had been left dead, and others wounded, on the battle field. Be that as it may, one of the color guard—Martin Mulvey—had brought off our regimental flag; which I at once caught up and waved, called on the boys to follow me, and, without orders, started back to meet the enemy. Those men never failed to respond to such a call, no matter what their condition if able to walk, nor did they then, but answered with a ringing cheer, and back we went in a slightly broken line composed not only of our regiment but of the entire division, with our flag at the most advanced point in the line; and kept on going, shooting and cheering until we had swept the enemy from the field, and the victory was won.

So, on the one hand, we have reliable witnesses that the incident occurred and, on the other, we have Harding saying he was the person waving the 31st battle flag. His statement is not proof, of course; but until contrary evidence is found, all future references to this incident should include his heroism at this moment of crisis. The historical process towards "truth" is based on new insights into what we think are facts. Many of the "facts" about the Civil War are based on personal narratives like Harding's, and we are fortunate to have now his exciting story to add to our data base. One wonders how many more narratives are still to be discovered.*

There is not yet any in-depth study of French Harding's life. This sketch below, based on county histories, tributes, obituaries, and other research, will highlight his life of public service.

Only a few details are known about French Harding's life before the Civil War. The third son of Joseph and Alice Elliott Harding, Joseph French Harding was born in Ellicott Mills, MD on November 9, 1838. His obituary mentions that the family emigrated to Iowa sometime early in his childhood, and the 1860 Census shows his sister Alice as having been born in Iowa in 1843. It also says Ida was born in Iowa and was eight years old, but that seems to conflict with the memoirs, where Harding mentions living from 1851 to 1852 in Newtown, VA. His father was a highway engineer, and the move after Newtown may have brought them to Randolph County to work on the continuing improvements to the Staunton and Parkersburg Turnpike and other roads in the 1850s. In *Mill Creek Memories*, a roster of students attending the Huttonsville Academy for the school year 1858-59 shows French, his two older brothers, George and Marion, and their sister Alice among the fifty-three students (p. 55). The 1860 Census notes those four Harding children, plus their

---

* Some readers may be interested in knowing how these memoirs were discovered. It started as a genealogy project. My late father's middle name was Harding, and his grandmother, Ida, was French Harding's sister. In a 1934 article in the Randolph County Historical Society magazine, I found a reference to these memoirs, and that led to contacting descendants in an effort to locate the manuscript. Subsequently, I found a fourteen page summary of the memoirs done in 1930 in the Roy Bird Cook collection at the Brockenbrough Library of the Museum of the Confederacy.

younger sister, Ida, were "attending school"—presumably all at the Huttonsville Academy. French and Marion are shown living with David C. Channel near Huttonsville in that year. An early tribute to Harding's character came in 1857 when Edward Kittle named his first-born son French Harding Kittle.

In this book, the story of the war years belongs to Harding, and I will only add at this point that all dates of major engagements he mentions correspond with those in Ashcraft's *31ˢᵗ Virginia Infantry* and Armstong's *19ᵗʰ and 20ᵗʰ Virginia Cavalry*. Of course, there were many occasions of detached service (away from the main regiment), and Harding's narrative may help historians and "buffs" better understand some of those smaller operations. Harding clearly had access to some histories of the Civil War, and, just as clearly, he did not like the fact that "history is written by the victors." His defense of Generals Lee and Early are most interesting in showing how this former company commander turned lawyer understood military and political strategy—from a Confederate perspective.

Harding was the kind of officer who was respected by most of his peers and subordinates; the kind generals picked for special assignments; but the kind majors and colonels would describe, in today's vernacular, as a "loose cannon," because they did not know what he might do next. Harding did not like what he perceived to be abuses of authority, and his narrative shows him to be aggressive both as a warrior and in defense of his men. After the war, and for the rest of his life, he was referred to as "Major Harding"—although there is no official record of a promotion to that rank.

In the memoirs he mentions spending some time near Corrick's Ford in Tucker County in the winter of 1865-66, and there are accounts that he was teaching after the war. The next milestone we can date precisely is his marriage to Luceba E. Wilmoth, daughter of Archibald and Caroline Taylor Wilmoth, on December 23, 1869. They had seven children. Two of their sons married two of Squire Newton Bosworth's daughters. Bosworth was a sergeant in

Company F, 31st VA infantry who kept an interesting diary for part of his war years. His entry for February 24, 1862 reads: "Went rabbit hunting this morning. Capt. Harding caught one a fair [race?]." This observation seems to support Harding's reputation for physical stamina and other skills necessary for outdoor life—and war.

In 1872 Harding was chosen to represent Randolph and its neighboring county, Tucker, at the West Virginia Constitutional Convention. This convention was called to correct some of the excesses of the 1862 constitution which, obviously, had been drafted during the war when the legalities of statehood were extremely uncertain and the partisan passions were high. As the unidentified writer of Harding's obituary put it:

> The people of this County reposing confidence in his character, integrity and ability—a confidence never displaced—drafted him into public service . . .

He held three more elected positions. In 1876 he ran against four other candidates and was elected Sheriff of Randolph County. When his term expired in 1881, he apparently began reading law, and his name first appears on court records as a lawyer in 1885. The Bar Association said at the time of his death in 1919:

> He brought to his career a well rounded active, mature mind, experienced in business and public affairs, with a reputation for honesty, uprightness and sterling worth and a nobility of character that brought to him a well-deserved goodly portion of professional business . . .

He practiced law in Beverly, then the county seat of Randolph, and in 1898, his oldest son, Clare Wilmoth Harding, became his partner. A lifelong Democrat, in 1886 Harding was again "drafted," this time to run for a seat in the House of Delegates representing Randolph and Tucker counties. In 1892 a small village west of Elkins was named

"Harding" in his honor. He was elected to serve another term in the House of Delegates in 1894, at a time when Republicans were winning most of the contests. According to his biography in Maxwell's *History of Randolph County*, "His election to every public office he has held was against his will and consent except that of Sheriff" (409).

Harding performed another piece of public service in May 1899. After a contested election to determine if the county seat should be moved to the new town of Elkins, the controversy came almost to be a shooting war, but cooler heads prevailed. "Major" Harding was one of the men representing Beverly on the peace commission which steered the controversy into the courts. The outcome favored Elkins, and Harding and his son moved their law office to the new county seat. An account of the courthouse feud can be found in Donald L. Rice's *Randolph 200*.

We can tell from internal evidence that Harding started writing the memoirs in 1917 and finished them the next year. We also know that he had a stroke on February 5, 1919, and died ten days later. This raises the question of the quality of his mind and memory at the time of writing. The 1916 *History of Randolph County* by Dr. A. S. Bosworth (nephew of Squire N. Bosworth) made this point: "Although several times wounded, Maj. Harding is today physically superior to the average man twenty years his junior" (350).

The Bar Association tribute stresses his mental powers:

> Regretted it has been that for a few years past his infirmity of hearing which he unnecessarily felt to be annoying to others, caused him to absent himself from the courtroom; but in his office, day by day, with the regularity of the sun, until ten days before his death, he toiled with mind undimmed and with the keenness of his faculties undiminished, for clientage that sought his sage wisdom in realization of the fact that the advice of Major Harding in his unswerving honesty was well worth having.

We would expect tributes and anonymous obituaries written by friends (or perhaps a family member) to be glowing, but the obituary was published on the front page of both county newspapers with his picture centered right below the headline. Clearly, Harding was considered a leading citizen of his community.

The tribute from the Bar Association contains these insights into Harding's character:

> In this professional tribute to a departed Brother, it is not unseemly that we also give testimony to Major Harding in his private life. Through all the years of his manhood, spent in this county, he was known as a man of exceptional purity and cleanliness in thought, speech, habits and conduct. Generous . . . charitable . . . faithful and true to duty . . . simple in his tastes . . . retiring in his manner, he craved not the plaudits or praise of the public; endowed with a rugged constitution in his glowing health he carried his burden of years with frame unbent and with head erect . . .

Finally, in typical turn-of-the century sentiment, the Bar tribute cites these two attributes of Harding's character:

> (1) In thoughts that spoke in his acts, in words that voiced the purity of his soul, in deeds that are monuments to his character, he exemplified the life of a Christian. . . . one of God's true noblemen.

> (2) Deprived of his tender life companion some years since [Luceba died in 1910], his soul bowed down in grief, still with manly fortitude, his outward life gave no sign of the loss he had suffered save that as each week rolled by his unfailing pathway led to her mortal resting place . . .

In the memoirs, we see French Harding (through his own eyes) as a kind of swashbuckling, youthful, Romantic warrior. The ca. 1863 letter in Appendix B lends credibility to his memory. But at the end of his life, we see him praised by the community for his modest demeanor, honorable character, public service, and weekly visits to his wife's grave—a kind of ideal Victorian gentleman. His life mirrors the cultural changes of our nation; and in both epochs, he was an exemplar.

French Harding's conduct during the war, and his honorable and productive life after it, suggests that he would not be the type to fabricate stories or claim glory for something he did not do. A few of his claims may not be true due to inadequate knowledge or misremembering, but it seems safe to assume this man of "unswerving honesty" was being truthful. That said, his insights, his command of detail, and his point of view as a company grade officer make these memoirs a valuable addition to our understanding of our Civil War.

If Harding did not crave the "plaudits or praise of the public," why did he write the memoirs at all? Few people nearing the age of 80—or any age—produce a 220 page manuscript without a burning desire to do so. At one point, he says he wanted his family to know his thoughts (180), and that may be the only answer this question needs. But several themes appear in the writing which reveal what parts of his story he wanted to emphasize.

The first is loneliness. The reader can note the many occurrences of this theme by referring to "Alone and/or loneliness" in the Index. A major part of Harding's war experience was losing his brothers and his close "chums," and he tries to suggest to us how he felt. This pathos works on the reader in a couple of ways: first, the losses suffered during the war, and then the "real time" in which he was writing the memoirs. His wife, Luceba, died in 1910, and he was outliving many of his comrades. As the obituary points out, Harding, at the time of his death, was one of only five survivors of the seventy eight members of the 1872 Constitutional Convention. Associated with this theme of loss and loneliness may have been the desire to memorialize in print those lost comrades who fought and died with him. There are existing samples of his willingness to write such tributes.

A second major theme is that of aggressiveness in battle. It is apparent in many of the anecdotes in the memoirs, and I have indexed where he specifically mentions his preference for chasing, rather than running from, the enemy (Harding, French: Aggressiveness). This trait sometimes got him into trouble with the bureaucracy, but his self-proclamations do not seem to be feigned. In fact, his attack on poor Captain Badger in Chapter XXXVI unintentionally reveals to us that some of that aggressiveness still existed in 1918—and it has a harsh edge not very flattering to Harding. The irony, of course, is that Badger's report contains a creditable statement of the respect his enemies had for Harding's prowess as a warrior.

Finally, there seems to be a theme of reconciliation that revolves around his frequent use of the word "Gallant" (see Index). He often invokes it when mentioning a comrade who died on the field of battle. He pointedly does not use it with Generals Sheridan, Hunter, or Fremont whose wartime actions he despised. Of course, it does not appear in his portrayal of Colonel Hoffman either. The use of the word "gallant," or something similar, in connection with Federal soldiers clearly signifies the kind of reconciliation that led to veterans groups of the opposing armies having reunions together. His admiration for the valor and decent behavior of the Federal soldiers (obviously characteristics of his own life) is contrasted with his attitude towards the unnamed person who "turned in" his brother George and the Radical Republicans who controlled the West Virginia government after the Civil War until 1870. A good example of this reconciliation is the friendship that develops between Harding and Sheriff Phares after the war.

The denouement (the final flurry of activity before a drama ends) of Harding's story reveals the beginnings of this reconciliation. On the day before he signs his own parole, Harding has an armed confrontation with the Sheriff. Phares defames Marion's memory, and Harding, with some risk, draws a pistol on him in the presence of Federal troops. The next day the Sheriff's father asks the Federal commander in Beverly to arrest Harding for shooting his son. Harding mollifies the old man (who reminds him of his own aging father) by saying empathetically that he understands his desire for revenge, but he will not apologize for any of his war-time actions because he was doing his duty. In both scenes of this drama, the authority figure is Captain Lafayette Bechtel (Harding uses the name "Beckel") of the Eighth Ohio Volunteer Cavalry. Harding calls him "one of nature's noblemen" (201) and gives him, on the second day, one of the three pistols. This highly symbolic gesture between warriors has multiple meanings (surrender or respect—depending on the circumstances). In this case, Harding's act resonates with both of those meanings, but Harding retains a measure of control by proffering Bechtel a choice of the three. And, in visual terms, Harding would still look like a warrior with his remaining weapons. This digression into literary analysis is to make the point that Harding was a very good and knowledgeable writer. With the additional scene of his homecoming, the sense of resolution and reconciliation that brings his Civil War story to an end is almost palpable.

Even if modern readers are uncomfortable with the lavish praise given to Harding upon his death, we can recognize that it contains undeniable evidence that he was highly thought of by many of his contemporaries. He was a leader, a teacher, and a counselor. People listened when Harding spoke, and now we get a chance to "hear" his story of valor and sacrifice during the Civil War. His is a grand remembrance.

Victor L. Thacker, Ph.D.
Elkins, WV 2000

Works Cited in Afterword

1860 Census of Randolph County, VA. (Copied from microfilm by Madeline W . Crickard, 1972).

Armstrong, Richard, L. *19th and 20th Virginia Cavalry.* Lynchburg, VA: H. E. Howard, Inc. 1994.

Ashcraft, John M., Jr. *31st Virginia Infantry.* Lynchburg, VA: H. E. Howard, Inc., 1988.

Bird, Mary, R.N. "Confederate Officers of Randolph County 1861 to 1865." *Randolph County Historical Society* 8 (1934): 10-16.

Bosworth, Dr. A. S. *History of Randolph County,* 1916; rpt. Parsons, WV: McClain Printing Co., 1975.

Gilmor, Colonel Harry. *Four Years in the Saddle.* New York: Harper, 1866.

Krick, Robert K. *Stonewall Jackson at Cedar Mountain.* Chapel Hill, NC: U. of North Carolina Press, 1990.

Maxwell, Hu. *History of Randolph County,* 1898; rpt. Parsons, WV: McClain Printing Co., 1991.

Obituary. "Brave Soldier and Splendid Citizen Answers Last Roll Call." Elkins, WV: *Randolph Enterprise,* Feb 20, 1919.

Randolph County Bar Association Tribute. *The Elkins Inter-Mountain,* February 22, 1919.

Rice, Donald L. *Randolph 200: A Bicentennial History of Randolph County, West Virginia, 1787-1987.* Waynesville, NC: Walsworth Publishing Co., Inc. 1987.

Russell, John. *Mill Creek Memories.* Parsons, WV: McClain Printing Co., 1995.

APPENDICIES

&

ADDITIONAL PHOTOGRAPHS

Luceba (1849-1910) and French (1838-1919)
HARDING
Married December 23, 1869
Photo ca. 1900

Reunion of Randolph County Confederate Veterans
From Virginia's 31st Infantry & 20th Cavalry
With the battle flag of the 31st Virginia Infantry
(early 1900s)

Marion (1837-1862) and French Harding
(ca. 1861)
&
Front page of Marion's Diary

224

Appendix A

Marion Harding
Civil War Diary
June 2nd, 1861-July 27th, 1861

[The existing manuscript is in bad condition. It is a 3" wide X 5 3/4" high notebook bound on the left side with string—only the bottom strand (of four) remains. It has no covers and page edges are ragged. The writing was done with a pencil. Some punctuation has been added for clarification. The dates are presented as Harding wrote them. The first page has this notation in some other person's hand:]

Marion Harding's Diary during the war.

A lock of his hair [missing]

Killed Oct 10, 1862 near Mingo Flats W. Va.

June 2nd

Left home, and went to Wm. Phares'. Hearing nothing relative to my company I left my gun and baggage at the store and went to meeting. My company not coming I stayed in the neighborhood all night.

June third

Started for Town. I met the company about two miles out on their way to meet the retreating army. We marched to the foot of Laurel hill where we halted for a
[bottom line of page missing] by command returned. On our return the alarm was given that an enemy was close upon our rear. By command of

225

our officers most of the company ran to the woods and took their stations near the road. I prepared to meet the enemy. The alarm proving false we left our ambush and again took up our line of march for Beverly. We had proceeded but a short distance when another alarm was given, which also proved false. We then went on until we reached [?] without further adventure. We quartered at the house of Mr. Earl [?]

June 4th—61

We still remain at head quarters waiting for further orders, our baggage wagons have gone on for safety. We are staying with the probability of being attacked—great excitement prevails. About four o clock we received orders to march up the road, our destination being kept secret. We quartered at Brown's store for the night.

[The next page has this entry:]
Due George Harding [older brother], for value rec'd. 3 dollars and fifty cents.

M. Harding
Nov. 1st 1860

June—5th

The troops are retreating from Beverly. They are now passing. They are under the supposition that Beverly will be taken this morning by the enemy. We are laying still awaiting further orders. Marched to Huttonsville and quartered at the house of Mr. Moses Hutton. Report says that the enemy in part have returned to Phillippi [sic].

June 6—61

Returned this morning from a scouting expedition in which I was engaged during a greater part of the night. We arrested a man whom we supposed to be a spy, but he was released by the officers as others are (I think) without a proper investigation. Nothing of importance is going on at this time. The army are quatered [sic] all along the road between H. [uttonsville?] and J. Stipe's. Rumor says they will return to Huttonsville.

June 7th—61

Nothing of importance has occurred since yesterday. I believe it is the intention to march on to Phillippi when sufficiently reinfforced [sic]. We have already received considerable reinforcements from Pochahontas. The troops have all returned to Huttonsville where they have gone into quarters.

June 8th—61

Today by vote of the company we were mustered into service. We are now a part and parcel of one of the armies of the Southern Confederacy. I sincerely hope we have espoused a good cause.

June 9th—61

Sabbath morning has come around and found us still in camp. Every thing is going on in camp as usual. No regard is paid to the Sabbath by the most of the army. Evening: Being tired of camp life I strolled off to a neighbors where I passed the day very pleasantly with my old friends, who also seemed glad to see me. The Army are apparently in very good spirits this evening. God protect the right.

June 10ᵗʰ—61

Stood guard last night and feel rather droopy this morning. A company of volunteers have just arrived from Greenbriar [sic]. Myself with nine others of our company have to stand as picket guards today and also tonight. There is great confusion and disorder in camp. I met one of the officers this evening who was surrounded by the fumes of alcohol. While we are thus governed by disipated [sic] men I fear we will not prosper.

June 11ᵗʰ—61

Stood guard nearly all night. One of guards shot at a man, but never could ascertain whether he hit him or not.

June 12—61

We were reinforced today with a very fine company from Hardy co. Every thing is going on quietly in camp. Nothing of special interest has occurred today.

June 13ᵗʰ—61

We are continually receiving reinforcements. The Co. from Hardy have for their drummer a little boy only eleven years of age. A sight of the little fellow seems to arouse the military spirit in the men. I think when we have received sufficient force it is the intention to march on to Phillippi.

June 14ᵗʰ—61

Left camp this morning and went down the river to my old boarding house where I was kindly received, and had twenty-five pies baked, which were a rare treat to our men. Returned to the camp in the evening, in time to see a fine company come in with a train of thirty odd waggons [sic] laden with provisions cannon & other munitions of war.

June 15—61

There has been a great deal of stir in camp today. We rec'd word at noon that we would have to march at seven o clock this evening. All are busy in making the necessary preparations . Where we are to march is, as yet, unknown. All we know is regard to the matter is that we start towards Phillippi under the command of Col. Jackson.

June 16th—61

We marched last night until about three o clock. We encamped a mile & half north of Beverly near the widow Colletts. Several of our men became so exhausted that they were unable to travel any farther. We started this morning about five oclock and traveled to the church below Hinkle's where we took about an hours rest & a bite to eat and started on our way.

We are now on top of Laurel hill just making preparations to move on. I believe it is the intention to try to surprise the enemy. Dinner is over and we are again on the march. It is now about sundown and we are encamped on the west side of Laurel hill with orders to sleep upon our arms. The intended movements are kept secret from the army. Some of our men are making tents out of brush as the appearance of the sky indicates rain.

June 17—61

This morning finds us still in camp waiting for reinforcements or at least from what I can learn I think that is the intention. From what I can learn [Break?] down the road towards the firing, and stationed in such a manner as to [fire?] at the cavalry in case of a retreat. This however was only for the enemy retreated upon the first firing. This is was thought was a ruse to draw our men into ambush but it did not have the desired effect so our men also returned toward camp. None of our men were killed. The enemy's loss were not ascertained; it is supposed the one or two were killed & some wounded. This evening we were reinforced by some seventeen hundred men who seem eager for fight. The troops are throwing up a redoubt or embankment in expecta[tion] of a attack from the enemy. Nothing further of importance has occurred today.

June 20th—61

They had another skirmish last night with the northern scouts. None of our men were killed. We do not know whether the enemy lost any or not. Report says has in fact moved up as far [as] Bealington [sic] where they have planted a cannon. We were reinforced today by about eight hundred men from Eastern Virginia who seemed anxious for fight. It is now near sundown & I am in a position from which I can see nearly all over camp. It presents a sight such as I never expect to see. Men, horses, tents, & waggons are to be seen in almost every direction.

June 21st

All was quiet last night in and around the camp.

Our camp is in a very pleasant place at the foot of Laurel Hill in Barbour County. Water is convenient and our situation is very desirable.

June 22nd—61

We had a terrible shower last night. The thunder echoed through the hills. The lightening flashed around & the wind blew violently dashing the rain through our little tents till some of our men were pretty well drenched with rain. The prisoners were taken to Beverly this morning as were also four guards who were found asleep at their posts. What the penalty will be in either case is unknown to me. Time however will reveal it. The report that the enemy have a cannon planted at Bealington is false. Our scouts were down the road last night six or eight miles. All was quiet. We have heard cannon firing repeatedly for the last three days. The place of firing has not yet been ascertained. Neither do we know for what purpose they have been firing.

The sun is sinking in the western horizon, calm but magnificent & gorgeous. It presents a striking contrast to the turmoil and strife in our camp. French and myself are now standing as sentinels in a position that overlooks the greater part of the camp.

23rd—61

Sunday morning
Stood guard last night about a mile & three-fourths below camp, All quiet & calm through night. We will have to stand guard all day. Sunday is the same as other days in war.

A Georgia Regiment [First Infantry] came in today between two & three o'clock. They numbered about one thousand. There were a good many negros among them. Their men appeared well armed and seemed anxious to meet the enemy. A man was buried today about four oclock. Supposed death resulted from an attack of apoplexy. Several guns were fired over his grave.

June 24th—61

Nothing of importance has occurred today. There are a good many sick men in camp, two or three in our own company.

June 25th—61

I am becoming a little tired of the dull monotony of camp life. I long for the society of those whom I have left behind. I feel quite indisposed this evening; have sent to the Dr. for medicine. They are digging another entrenchment near our camp along the foot of Laurel Hill.

26th—61

Feel better this morning but not yet fit for duty. Walked around camp this evening. The work of fortifying is progressing rapidly. I think the batteries are proof against small cannon. One of the sentinels near our camp fired upon a supposed spy this after-noon about five oclock, who it is supposed he missed. Twenty-eight of our men, together with Capt. Went as a guard today, to guard a grain waggon. They have just returned tired and hungry.

June 27—61

A sad accident happened today in camp. The seargent [sic] of the guard had placed a sentinel at the certain post with instructions not to let any person pass along a particular place. He was ordered not to halt any person whom he might see at that place, but fire upon first sight. He then left him, went off, took off his pistol and coat and then went to the spot which he had cautioned the sentinel to watch. The sentinel true to his orders fired upon him killing him instantly. The ball struck him on the left side & passed through his body near the heart. Name, Charles Harris from Louisa Co., Eastern Va.

June 28th—61

Another accident happened today; a man shot himself through the hand. I learned that the man who was shot yesterday was not a seargent as I had first heard, but only a private who gave the orders to the other sentinel that he said were given to him.

June 29—61

We rec'd our tents & blankets today which we consider a very valuable acquisition, as they were greatly needed. Their seems to be an inclination on the part of the company not to take muskets which they are requested to do.

June 30th—61

This morning seems to be in unison with the affairs of our country, being a dark and gloomy morning. We rec'd orders to move our quarters and went down to the main encampment and pitched our tents. Two of our [men] went off this morning. Suspisions [sic] being entertained that they had deserted. A party of cavalry were sent in pursuit of them.

July 1st—61

Our company seem very well satisfied with their new situation, yet there seems to be a general feeling of discontent on account of having to change our rifles for muskets which we did this morning though with a good deal of unwillingness. Our two men were brought in today by the cavalry and are now under guard in the camp. I sincerely pity them.

July 2nd—61

Today one month ago I left home to meet my company. I was down to see our prisoners this morning and took them some breakfast. They were taken at Henry Harper's two miles & a half above town. We started about four oclock this evening on expedition down the road to scout and stand guard. We are now between three and four miles below camp, waiting for further orders from Colonel, who has taken command of us himself.

July 3rd—61

Nothing was seen or heard of the enemy last night. When we came to camp this morning we were informed that a part of a regiment had been sent to the aid of Col. Heck's company, upon whom it was supposed an attack was contemplated.

July 4th—61

This morning we heard the report of several

cannon supposed to be fired by the enemy in commemoration of the fourth. Our Cavalry fired upon the enemy today. I was informed by them they wounded two of the enemy. Nothing further of importance has occurred today.

July 5th—1861

Our cavalry had a skirmish with the Northern scouts. They wounded one of them, and lost one of their own horses. Nothing further of importance has occurred.

July 6—61

We are sent out on a scout again. We are now about four miles below camp. A young man died in camp today. Disease supposed to be Pneumonia. He has two brothers in the army who seem to take his death very hard.

July 7th—61

We saw nothing of the enemy last night. But the alarm was given this morning about nine oclock that they were approaching. The Georgia regiment with part of the cavalry hastened down the road. Shortly after they had gone we heard the report of firearms. Tis now late in the evening, an irregular fire still continues. We have learned that some of the enemy have been killed. Number not known. One of our men wounded.

July 8—61

We were sent out last night to guard a [pass or field?] that leads into camp and are still out now at eight oclock. The fire was kept up at intervals during the night and at still continues. We have

learned that some have been killed. Number not
known. It is now about sundown. The firing has
continued all day. The enemy have fired several
cannon, with what result we do not know.

July 9th—61

The heavy firing we heard last night was from our
own men who repulsed the enemy, it is rumored
with considerable loss. We were ordered to camp
this morning where we stayed until noon. Part of
our company with others were then ordered out to
fall timber in order to prevent the enemy from
planting cannon on a hell that had command of
our camp. We had been there about three hours
when an alarm was given that the enemy were
upon us. We were commanded to leave
immediately and hasten into camp. Some of our
men, myself included, had reached the road when
the enemy begin [sic] to thro[wing] boom-shells
into our camp. The shells had to be thrown over
us, and one of them bursted in the air almost over
the heads of [two?] of our men. However we all got
safe into camp. They continued to throw the shells
until our men took one of their cannon down the
road and gave them a few rounds which silenced
them. They then attempted to take our cannon but
were promptly met by one of regiments who
repulsed them and [?] them to rout. Their loss not
known. Ours, Ours none.

July 10th—61

Nothing further was heard from the enemy last
night. We had a good night's rest and about ten
oclock this morning were called to take our stand
near our old position, about three quarters of a
mile from camp. It is thought that the enemy may
probably try to pass to camp by the road which we

now hold. It is now about midday. Since I commenced writing, the enemy have again begun to throw shells into camp. I have just now learned that the enemy have planted a cannon on the hill on which we were chopping yesterday. I with five others were sent this afternoon a short distance from camp in the direction of the enemy. We are in a corn crib near a house when a young man whom we had sent to the house for water returned hastily without the water with the news that some of the enemy were approaching. We ran out with our guns in our hands and saw two men passing through a field towards our pickets. They continued to advance until they reached the brow of hill where our pickets fired upon them. The men returned the fire, and then one of them ran. Our pickets continued to fire. The other man fell and lay for about ten minutes and then crawled down the hill out of sight. We learn that another was killed, at the same time a little in the rear of the two we saw. The enemy threw several shells into camp this evening but did no injury. Our guards took a prisoner this evening, supposed to be a spy.

July 11th—61

Our pickets and the enemy still keep firing at each other. We are still stationed in the woods where we were yesterday. I have been placed out as a picket guard for to night at some distance from our company.

12—61

Was taken off guard last night about nine oclock. Our whole com.[pany] was hastened into camp when we were informed that we had to march towards Beverly as the enemy had routed Col. Heck's troops and were on there (sic) way to

Beverly. We marched on untill we reached the cross road at Geo. Wards. Hearing that the enemy were in strong force so near that we could not pass B.[everly], we took up the Leading-Creek road. We marched on to J. Kalars leaving a great deal of our baggage & some waggons along the road.

July—13—61

Started early this morning to try to reach the Northwestern Pike. We had got as far as the second crossing below Kalars when we learned that the enemy were in pursuit and had attacked us in the rear. General Garnett rode back and while at the head of his men was shot down just as he ordered our men to retreat. Our men used their cannon very successfully, killing and wounding a good many of the enemy. But were at length forced to retreat after having repulsed the enemy. Once it was at the second attack that the retreat was ordered. Our regiment was drawn up into line of battle to await the approach of the enemy, but for some reason unknown to us we were again ordered to march forward. Then commenced a most precipitous retreat. All our baggage was thrown away. The loss we sustained was immense, that is [in] property.

July 13th

We traveled last night untill two Oclock and then lay down on our guns in the woods having had scarcely anything to eat all day yesterday. We were very much exhausted. We were aroused after having slept an hour or two and started on without any breakfast. The men were so hungry that they ate bark and leaves off of the shrubs. A little after midday we halted, had some beef killed and roasted it on sticks. As soon as we had eaten a bite we started, though the men were so worn down that we left them strung all along the road. We missed one of our men yesterday and two today.

July 14th—61

We traveled last night untill about two o clock when we halted for a while and then started on again without breakfast. We traveled on for two or three miles and then halted and ____ something to eat. We are traveling through Hardy Co. having left Maryland yesterday. We left a good many men along the road today. It is reported that the Yankees are still taking [up] our men who lag behind. Traveled all day (on one meal the first for several day). [We] halted at two O clock at night. We are now in Petersburg, a small town near the centre of the County.

July 17—61

We have been so driven about & harrassed [sic] that I have lost a day or two and got the wrong date. However the main features are right. For some reason unknown to us as still have to march in the night. Report says that the enemy are still in pursuit. Traveled last night untill midnight. Passed from Hardy into Pendleton. Came on about twelve miles this morning before we had anything to eat. We then stopped and took a dinner prepared for us by the citizens. The best we have had for sometime. We have just crossed the South Branch and are now encamped in a beautiful valley—South Branch.

July 18th

We started last evening about five—and came as far [as] Franklin, a distance of 13 miles. Arived [sic] here about midnight. We stay'd in Franklin today untill about four Oclock. Franklin is a small town near the South-Branch. The people here are very hospitable, and true to the state. Started this evening at four and traveled about thirteen mile. Stopped about midnight on the waters of South Branch.

July 19th

Started early this morning & came to Monterey eleven miles from where we camped last night. There are about three thousand soldiers in M.[onterey] besides our own army. We have not fully learned [the] loss we sustained at the fight and along the road. General Garnett was killed at the fight on Cheat

20th—61

The soldiers who were cut off at the fight on Cheat are still coming in. The number missed at that time I was told amt. to about seven hundred, very few of whom were killed. There are still a good many missing. The fight took place at Corricks ford. We are still in camp at Monterey. A good many of the prisoners taken at the fight on Rich Mt. Came in today. They were exchanged for northern prisoners.

July 21st—61

Nothing of special interest has occurred to day. The Georgians who were cut off are still coming in. We have heard heavy cannonading today, appeared to be in the direction of Winchester. There are several cases of measels [sic] in camp. Feel somewhat indisposed myself. Two new volunteers today, Thomas Lewis & [John F.] Taylor.

July 22nd

Marshall Kittle joined our company today. We were reinforced by a regiment from Arkansas. The firing we heard on yesterday was at the Manassa [sic] Junction. A dispatch came in today with the news that there was a heavy battle there in which we were victorious, particulars not known. Supposed a vast numbers were killed. Wet and gloomy today.

July 23rd—61

Stood guard today. We were reinforced today by three regiments containing in all about twenty-six hundred men. Nothing further heard from the battle at Mannassa [sic].

July 24th—61

Heard today that we obtained a decisive victory at Mannassa. One of our men came I today whom we have not seen since the day we retreated __________ the enemy and made a very narrow escape.

July 25th

We started this morning in the direction of _____ taking the Staunton & Parkersburg pike. We are now halted on the side of the [road] _____ about eleven miles from where we started. We will stay here for the night.

July 26—61

We are still in camp on this side of the Alleghany where we stopped yesterday. How long we will stay here is unknown to us. Several waggon loads of prisoners liberated passed by today.

July 27—61

Still in camp _____ every thing is [going] on as usual. Nothing of importance has occurred for two or three days.

[This is the end of M. Harding's daily entries.]

Page 60. [of the original diary contains the following entries:]
June 14th 1861

	$	Cts
Loaned W.[alter V.] Lewis		25
June 20th Loaned W. Lewis		30
" 20th J[ames R.] Apperson		15

Page 61.

And while we listen Lord
To Holy truths divine
Speak, Savior, speak the gracious word
Oh, whisper we are thine.
         M. Harding

Page 62.

My heart to Thee I now resign
Tis all dear Savior I can give
Thou knowest I would be wholy thine
With Thee I would forever live.

Oh, Save me from the power of
[Hell?] [and] from every evil flee
Then may I Lord my Kingdom win

And there forever live with thee.

Oh may this be my constant aim
To win a crown of life above
The Kingdom of my Savior gain
Bask in the sunlight of thy love.

Then from all sin and sorrow free
The praises of my God I'll sing
And all thy ransomed host with me
Will make the vault of Heaven ring.

Page 63. [Top half of page is cut out; bottom is blank.]

Page 64. [Top half is missing; Bottom contains in large, elaborate script]:

Randolph Co.
Barbour County

Page 65. [This page just contains two names]:

A.[sa] Kelley
P. or D.[udley] Long

Page 66.
Members of Mess

1. Branch M. Robertson
2. A. S. Ward
3. J. F. Harding
4. Marion Harding
5. Joseph Stipe
6. Wm. Stipe
7. L.D. Westfall
8. Absalom Shiflett

    9. Wm. H. Wilson
  10. Cyrus Crouch
  11. O.H.P. Lewis
  12. Walter Lewis
  13. Asa Kelly
  14. Eugenius Hutton

Pages 67, 68, & 69 [contain numerical calculations.]

Page 70. [This appears to be a statement for Marion's work as a teacher—probably in the New Interest (now Kerens, W. Va.) area as mentioned in French Harding's memoirs.] $106.76

Whole amt. of school bill for the term ending March 1st, 1861. One hundred & six dollars, and seventy six cents.

6 1/4 X 6 1/4=25/4 X 25/4=625/16=39 1/16

Page 71. [In the top half of page, a column of numbers (not added) and his signature]:

125
126
150
110
 25
120
115

Marion Harding

Page 72. [On this page is what appears to be a list of students (with grades in the right column?) from the New Interest (now Kerens, W. Va.) area. Student # 16 is the 12 year old girl that French Harding describes in his memoirs. He marries her eight years later.]

1.	Solomon George	81
2.	Francis M. Taylor	61
3.	P. [H.?] McLean	54
4.	John S. Day	10
5.	Elias Vanscoy	9
6.	Alba Stalnaker	18
7.	William Vanscoy	53
8.	Elijah Channell	56
9.	Adam Corrick	65
10.	Barton [?] Corrick	22
11.	Gilbert Hart	71
12.	Martha C[?] Hart	5
13.	Martha Schoonover	6
14.	Susannah [?] Schoonover	11
15.	William Simmons	58
16.	Luceba Wilmoth	77
17.	[?] Wilmoth	79
18.	[O. H. ?] Vanscoy	46
19.	[?] Vanscoy	22

Page 73. [This page of the existing manuscript has a left hand column with ditto marks in it, and a right hand column with numbers in it which probably have something to do with Marion's teaching duties in the Spring of 1861.]

Page 74. [The last page of the diary appears to be another set of grades, perhaps for the above students; but it is very faded and stained.]

[The same day Marion Harding died, a son was born to Capt. Jacob Currence, first commander of Company F. Currence named the boy Marion Harding Currence.]

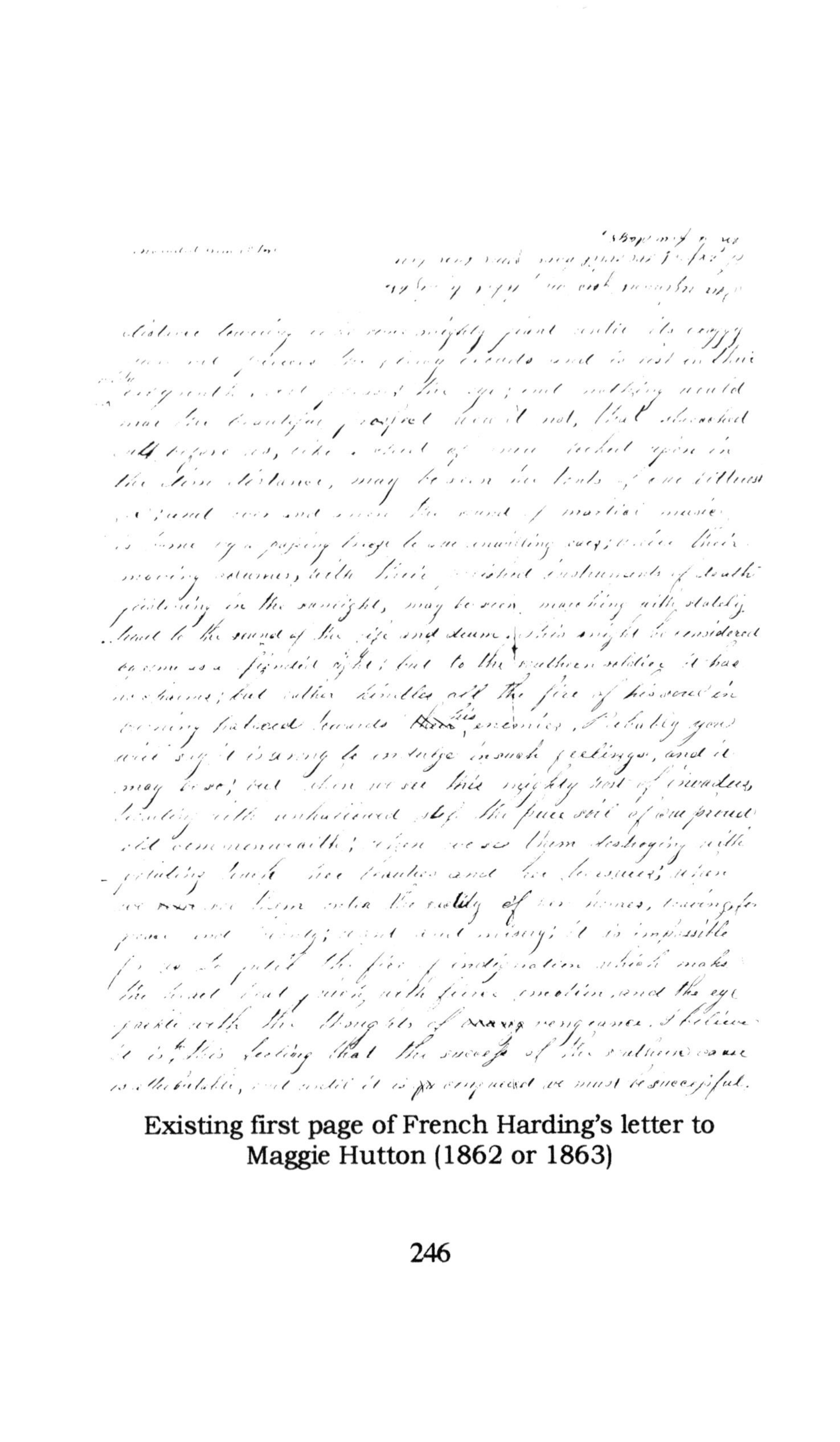

Existing first page of French Harding's letter to
Maggie Hutton (1862 or 1863)

Letter from French Harding to Maggie Hutton
(1862 or 1863)

[The first page (or more) seems to be missing. There is no salutation or date, and the first page of the existing manuscript (MS) starts in mid-sentence

Page 1

[on top left: "concluded from 4th page"; under that notation is an embossed watermark with the name "Croton" in the center of it]

[on top right—and upside down]: "Our regiment goes on picket tonight. I expect we will have some fun here in a few days."

[The existing MS begins here]:

distance towering like some might giant until its craggy summit pierces the fleecy clouds and is lost in their misty labyrinth. All pleases the eye; and nothing would mar the beautiful prospect were it not, that streached [sic] out before us, like a sheet of snow looked upon in the dim distance, may be seen the tents of our bitterest foe; and ever and anon the sound of martial music is borne by a passing breeze to our unwilling ears; while their moving columns, with their polished instruments of death glistening in the sunlight, may be seen marching with stately tread to the sound of the fife and drum. This might be considered by some as a splendid sight; but to the southern soldier it has no charms; but rather kindles all the fire of his soul in burning hatred towards his enemies. Probably you will say it is wrong to indulge in such feelings, and it may be so, but when we see this mighty host of invaders, treading with unhallowed step the pure soil of our proud old commonwealth; when we see them destroying with poluting [sic] touch her beauties and her treasures; when we see them enter the sactity [sic] of her homes, leaving, for peace and plenty; want and misery; it is impossible for us to quell the fire of indignation which maks [sic] the heart beat quick with fierce emotion, and the eye sparkle with the thoughts of vengeance. I believe it is to this feeling that the success of the southern cause is attributable, and until it is conquered we must be successful.

Page 2

[on the top of this page (upside down) and then down the left hand margin: "Write me a good long letter as soon as you can and give me the news generally. Please let me know how fathers family are Lizzie was sick when I last heard from home. Tell Margaret that I am well. She seems to have entirely forgotten me."]

Rumors of foreign intervention still abound; and all of our most learned and dignified croakers give it as their decided opinion that France will ere long acknowledge the independence of the confederate states; for my part, I don't know much about such things and care less. I think the surest plan is to depend upon our own resources. I am confident they are sufficient to meet our wants and feel certain if southern skill and bravery is not equal to the task before them, it is no use for France to offer her feeble assistance. Our forces have lately captured several of the enemy's gunboats. Peace still keeps in the distance; does not seem any closer today than it did a year ago, though it may come sooner than we expect it. The Yankeys [sic] on the other side of the river seem willing to lay aside their arms, and persue [sic] a more proffitable [sic] and pleasant occupation; and I know we are willing for them to do so. I do not mean that we would be willing to receive peace on any terms, Never! We are not willing to surrender any cherished rights; not willing to give up one foot of

Southern soil; would rather die on the battle field, fighting for our homes and friends, than to see them in the hands of the enemy; would die on the field of battle rather than to become the tyrants slave; yet—peace together with liberty would be hailed with joy, and many a heart would bound high with the rapturous thought of returning to his cherished home, where he knows anxious friends with praying hearts and tearful eyes await his coming with untold of emotions of joy.

Page 3

[on the top of this page (upside down) and then down the left hand margin: "Tell Ginnie I received her interesting letter and will answer it as soon as I have a sufficient stack of news on hand to make it acceptable. Remember me to all inquiring friends and tell them I would take it as a better proof of friendship if they would write to me occasionally and let me know they are getting along these troublesome times."]

I sometimes think our long absence will make us appreciate home more highly than we did befor [sic] we knew its loss; and I believe it will be pleasant to remember the hardships and dangers that we are now called upon to pass through; and when we are permitted to return home in peace; when the sound of the cannon is no longer heard to disturb the peaceful quiet of our <u>homes</u>; telling by its harsh sound of widows and orphans being made; of parents bereft of their children; when we can gather of a beautiful evening as the twilight gathers in the shaddows [sic] of the west, in the family circle, around the hearthstone; then our happiness would be complete were it not that there will be some loved one gone from that circle; one link broken that cannot be reunited, and our minds will wander from the living to the dead who are sleeping calmly in the quiet graves perhaps the victim of desease [sic], or else have fallen in defence [sic] of their country. There is no friendly hand to plant the blossoms around their tombstone, or tongue to sing their funeral dirge; but they lie unheeded in their glory; and there—

> "Honor come a pilgrim gray
> To keep the turf that wraps their clay,
> And freedom will a while repair
> To dwell a weeping hermit there."*

I would love dearly to pay old Randolph a visit this fall, I love the dear old place, with it crystal waters sparkling in the forests as they wind hither and thither among the mountains seeking some outlet to the river; and those hills, which the stranger would pronounce uncomly [sic] in

Page 4

their appearance are beautiful to me; in them my boyhood was passed and, I love them still; it was my delight to wander through the mountains where I could chase the flying deer as it bounded like some fairy thing over hill and valley; stop to cull some beautiful flower that grew in my pathway; or seek the secluded summit of some rugged hill where I could meet the lightnings [sic] glance eye to eye and revel in its dazzling brightness. I expect you will call this weakness in me; perhaps it is, and I will change the subject.

I heard from Seymour Phares and George Bradley a short time since. George had been sick but was nearly well again; they are enjoying themselves as well as could be expected under the circumstances, and say they would rather be where they are than in the southern army. I am willing to let them have choices. Company "F" are all well and in fine spirits; ready to meet the yanks, at any time.

The "old man" (Billy) [Smith] is well, and has for some time been looking for a letter from a certain lady living near Huttonsvill [sic] , who revels in the interesting appellation

---

* William Collins, "Ode Written in the Year 1746" (stanza 2)

of Miss Maggie Hutton. He seems inclined to believe that he has been forgotten; and talks vehemently about getting a divorce; and turning his attention to Miss—Miss—well a Miss somebody living in the famous County of <u>Randolph</u>, probably you can guess her name. She has dark brown hair and, laughing blue eyes that makes a fellows heart jump up into his throat every time he encounters them; has a peculiar winning way which plays smash with the hart [sic] that is not 'void of susceptability [sic]; and renders her a dangerous competitor. Lieutenants Perry and Dud are both well. Dud says he will be much obliged to you for your letter when he gets it; he thinks it will certainly have something very interesting in it or it would not be so long coming. Perry still remains very complimentary to school teachers, and seems to give them a decided preference. I would not be surprised if one of them gets a piece of paper from him, with certain peculiar marks upon it, signifying that he is tired of living alone, and calling upon her to accompany him over the checkered pathway of life.

Adam seems very much concerned about the mill and is continually wondering whether it is still able to grind or not. As for William [?] he thinks that every sound that breaks upon the stillness of the night is the chirping of some stray cricket (Crickard) or the roaring of Shavers Run.

But I suppose it is useless for me to dwell longer on the feelings of Company "F", as the large amount of letters written have no doubt made them known before this time. I must close my uninteresting letter, So—hoping to hear from you soon; and wishing you all the happiness allotted to mortals in this troublesome world, I remain—Maggie, your friend French—

[Note: on this page, and this page only, French is clearly trying to demarcate paragraphs. I have indicated where by double spacing in this text. On this last page,

French's handwriting gets very small as he realizes he is running out of space. His name is squeezed into the bottom right-hand corner. Apparently he then goes to pages 1,2, and 3 of the MS and adds his final comments in the margins.]

Sheridan's Ride
By
Thomas Buchanan Read

Up from the South at break of day,
Bringing to Winchester fresh dismay,
The affrighted air with a shudder bore,
Like a herald in haste, to the chieftain's door,
The terrible grumble, and rumble, and roar,
Telling the battle was on once more,
        An Sheridan twenty miles away.

And wider still those billows of war
Thundered along the horizon's bar;
And louder yet into Winchester rolled
The roar of that red sea uncontrolled,
Making the blood of the listener cold,
As he thought of the stake in that fiery fray,
        With Sheridan twenty miles away.

But there is a road from Winchester town,
A good, broad highway leading down;
And there, through the flush of the morning light,
A steed as black as the steed of night
Was seen to pass, as with eagle flight;
As if he knew the terrible need,
He stretched away with his utmost speed;
Hills rose and fell; but his heart was gay,
        With Sheridan fifteen miles away.

Still sprung from those swift hoofs, thundering South,
The dust, like smoke from the cannon's mouth;
Or the trail of a comet, sweeping faster and faster.
Foreboding to traitors the doom of disaster,
The heart of the steed and the heart of the master
Were beating like prisoners assaulting their walls,

Impatient to be where the battlefield calls;
Every nerve of the charger was strained to full play,
      With Sheridan only ten miles away.

Under his spurning feet the road
Like an arrowy Alpine river flowed,
And the landscape sped away behind
Like an ocean flying before the wind,
And the steed, like a barque fed with furnace ire,
Swept on, with his wild eye full of fire.
But lo! He is nearing his heart's desire
He is snuffling the smoke of the roaring fray,
      With Sheridan only five miles away.

The first that the general saw were the groups
Of stragglers, and then the retreating troops;
What was done? What to do? A glance told him both,
Then, striking his spurs, with a terrible oath,
He dashed down the line 'mid a storm of huzzas,
And the wave of retreat checked its course there, because
The sight of the master compelled it to pause.
With foam and with dust the black charger was gray;
By the flash of his eye, and the red nostri'ls play,
He seemed to the whole great army to say,
"I have brought Sheridan all the way
      From Winchester down to save the day!"

Hurrah! Hurrah for Sheridan
Hurrah! Hurrah for horse and man!
And when their statues are placed on high,
Under the dome of the Union sky,
The American soldier's Temple of Fame;
There with the glorious general's name,
Be it said, in letters both bold and bright,
      "Here is the steed that saved the day,
By carrying Sheridan into the fight
      From Winchester twenty miles away!"